Charting Women's Journeys

Critical Perspectives on Crime and Inequality

Critical Perspectives on Crime and Inequality presents cutting edge work informed by these schools of thought: feminism, peacemaking criminology, left realism, Marxism, cultural criminology, and postmodernism. In an age of instrumental reason and increasing state control, the need for critical and independent analysis of power and social arrangements has never been more acute. Books published in this series will be monographs for scholars and researchers, as well as texts for course use.

Titles in Series:

The Politics of Organized Crime and the Organized Crime of Politics, by Alfredo Schulte-Bockholt

Advancing Critical Criminology: Theory and Application, edited by Walter S. DeKeseredy and Barbara Perry

Symbolic Gestures and the Generation of Global Social Control, by Dawn Rothe and Christopher W. Mullins

Charting Women's Journeys, by Judith Grant

Charting Women's Journeys

From Addiction to Recovery

JUDITH GRANT

LEXINGTON BOOKS

A division of
ROWMAN & LITTLEFIELD PUBLISHERS, INC.
Lanham • Boulder • New York • Toronto • Plymouth, UK

LEXINGTON BOOKS

A division of Rowman & Littlefield Publishers, Inc.
A wholly owned subsidiary of The Rowman & Littlefield Publishing Group, Inc.
4501 Forbes Boulevard, Suite 200
Lanham, MD 20706

Estover Road
Plymouth PL6 7PY
United Kingdom

British Library Cataloguing in Publication Information Available

Library of Congress Cataloging-in-Publication Data

Grant, Judith, 1942–
Charting women's journeys : from addiction to recovery / Judith Grant.
p. cm. — (Critical perspectives on crime and inequality)
Includes bibliographical references and index.
ISBN-13: 978-0-7391-1478-0 (cloth : alk. paper)
ISBN-10: 0-7391-1478-6 (cloth : alk. paper)
1. Women drug addicts—Appalachian Region. 2. Women alcoholics—Appalachian Region. 3. Women drug addicts—Rehabilitation—Appalachian Region. 4. Women alcoholics—Rehabilitation—Appalachian Region. I. Title.
HV4999.W65G73 2008
362.29082'0974—dc22 2007045647

Printed in the United States of America

The paper used in this publication meets the minimum requirements of American National Standard for Information Sciences—Permanence of Paper for Printed Library Materials, ANSI/NISO Z39.48–1992.

I dedicate this book to the rural Appalachian women whom I interviewed for this study along with the Canadian women of the Women and Substance Abuse Project. Both groups of women taught me much about bravery, about courage, and about the ability to overcome obstacles in life. I also dedicate this book to the professors in the Department of Women's Studies at York University in Toronto, Ontario, Canada, who taught me how important it is to afford women the opportunities for their voices and experiences to be heard.

Contents

Foreword

Addiction among women continues to be a vexing social problem with no clear solution. Individuals, families, and social organizations use various approaches to end addiction ranging from social isolation and family enmeshment to formal detox programs, but results remain uneven. In this study of the recovery careers of female addicts living in rural settings, Judith Grant explores the ways in which twenty-five addicts engage in individual processes of self-recovery. While eighteen women used the help of formal institutional recovery programs such as Alcoholics Anonymous and Narcotics Anonymous and eight did not, all succeeded in ending their addictive careers by reconstituting themselves. Using feminist methods of inquiry and a Meadian theoretical framework of analysis, Grant follows women through three distinct recovery phases as they slowly come to shift their understandings of themselves, others, and their social objects: addiction. Central to a recovery lies a process by which women reinvent themselves by altering their involvement with themselves, their partners, friends, children, and of course their addictive substance. This book offers concrete solutions for policy makers and provides a refreshing measure of hope for the largely invisible population of individuals, both family members and addicts, who suffer terribly from this disease.

Dr. Nancy Mandell
Associate Professor
Sociology and Women's Studies
York University
Toronto, Ontario, Canada

Preface

This book is based on my interest evolving from my work with women previously addicted to alcohol and/or drugs. From 1994 through 1997, I was the researcher and educator for a Canadian community project (the Women and Substance Abuse Project, WASA) working with 300+ women formerly addicted to substances.[1] My job was to establish programs to help women create alternative lifestyles for themselves. As I worked with these women, I became especially interested in the social, individual, and cultural forces that shaped women's addiction and recovery. Many times I asked them, "So, how did you get here?" meaning, "How did you get into recovery?" Their answers were varied, yet similar.

The women's stories of their recovery experiences revealed the use of certain strategies that helped them recover from addiction: geographically moving from where they formerly had lived, rebuilding structures in their lives with strong ties to the nonaddicted social world, establishing new relationships and reestablishing previous relationships with family, children, partners, and friends who were not addicted to alcohol and/or drugs.

Through ongoing interaction within sober environments, these women afforded themselves opportunities to adopt new meanings about themselves and to construct new lives as women no longer addicted. As they related their stories of addiction, I began to understand that their use of alcohol and/or drugs had involved experimentation, pleasure, and compatibility with other users in ways that were meaningful to them. However, I had little information on the social processes that had propelled these women into addiction in the first place. Nor did I know the social nature of women's recovery or the factors involved in how women see themselves as they process their changes from addiction to recovery. How do they perceive, think about, and create lines of action? How do they interact and reflect upon the ways in which they make meanings of such processes for themselves? How do women make sense of their meanings toward an object, such as alcohol and/or drugs, that once was so important in their lives? In my work with the WASA women, it was obvious that addiction/recovery involved profound changes in their selves as well as changes for significant others in their lives. Therefore, I am especially interested in how women process such changes.[2]

To better understand the social processes through which rural[3] women in this study shift from the role of addict to that of nonaddict, I divide their experiences into three analytically distinct phases: (1) *The Preaddicted Self*, (2) *The Addicted Self*, and (3) *The Recovering Self*. *The Preaddicted Self* pertains to the preexperimental phase in which social processes in women's lives lead them to experiment with alcohol and/or drugs for various reasons and on various levels. *The Addicted Self* refers to the processes whereby these women become immersed in an alcohol and/or drug culture and develop concepts of themselves as addicts. *The Recovering Self* refers to the processes by which women begin to consider recovery and struggle to stay abstinent. These three phases are not necessarily empirically separate or temporally sequential. The paths to self-conceptions as addicts and, subsequently, as nonaddicts vary among women in this study.

Incorporating who women are, what they think and feel, how they come to be addicted, and what pressures and social challenges affect their lives, I offer in this study an understanding of how rural Appalachian women, through their interactions with selves and others, create social structures in their lives that in turn shape their behaviors in processes of addiction and recovery.[4]

Many individuals helped in the creation of this book. It would not have been possible without the help and assistance of the rural Appalachian women I interviewed. I thank them for sharing with me their memories of what it "was like for them," as they moved from addiction to recovery. Their answers to my many questions were testaments to women's courage and creativity in escaping addiction. Hopefully, their documented voices will encourage other women as they struggle to enter recovery.

I express my gratitude to several scholars who provided critical and positive responses to my work: Dr. Nancy Mandell, Dr. Patricia Evans, and Dr. Rina Cohen. I also want to thank Dr. Walter DeKeseredy for his advice and encouragement as he tactfully encouraged me to turn my research into a book. And for making sure the book has the proper commas, etc., I thank my editor, Rick Huard, for his skillful editing.

Special gratitude goes to my friend Dr. Anna Wagner-Ott for her encouragement and continuous positive reinforcement along with the wonderful conversations we had that kept me going as my study unfolded. Mary Louise Luck was a guiding light as she taught me to trust myself in all aspects of my professional life and to her I say, "Thank you."

Further appreciation goes to my husband, Adrian, who was my rock of strength during the time I struggled with my work. He continuously kept me focused and provided the moral support I needed to finish. And, finally, a special thank-you goes to my children, Jennifer and Matthew, who always stated how proud they were and are of their academic mother.

Notes

1. The WASA Project was funded by the Health and Promotions Branch, Health Canada, and was sponsored by the Advisory Council on the Status of Women, Moncton; Crossroads for Women, Inc., Moncton; and Support to Single Parents, Inc., Moncton, New Brunswick, Canada, during the years 1994 through 1997.

2. As I was leaving the WASA Project, one of the WASA women stated to me: "Judith, go tell our stories." Therefore, in this book I undertake to "tell" women's stories of their addiction and recovery processes, thus incorporating both my previous community work and my research interests.

3. My definition of the term "rural" is taken from Websdale's suggestion that "rural," as a descriptive term, is "commonly understood to refer to the countryside or small towns as opposed to cities" and is "not simply a physical place but a social place as well." See N. Websdale, *Rural Women Battering and the Justice System: An Ethnography* (Thousand Oaks, CA: Sage, 1998), 36; R. Weisheit, D. Falcone, and E. R. Wells, "Community Policing in Small Town and Rural America," *Crime and Delinquency* 40 (1994): 564.

4. This research evolved while I was teaching at a small eastern university in the United States from 2001–2005. This gave me the opportunity to hear the stories and gather interviews from the rural Appalachian women within the area where I was teaching. This book is a result of that research study.

Introduction

> It is time to recognize the fact that because of drug use many girls and women have been robbed of their identity, their dignity, their quality of life, and their right to protection. It is time to review our development paradigm and strategies, as well as our approaches to the drug issue, in order to make a real change and one that will enable women who are affected by the drug problem to reclaim their humanity and their rights.[1]

This book is about the meaning of addiction and recovery in the lives of twenty-five rural Appalachian women who have been practicing abstinence from the use of alcohol and/or drugs for eighteen months or more in a small rural community in the United States. The empirical focus is on the ways in which these women's lives have been transformed through the processes of addiction to and abstinence from these substances.

Although a vast body of literature has developed during the past twenty years on substances, addiction, and treatment, little attention has been given to the complexities of rural women's lives as they enter and exit addiction, the meanings of addiction for them, and how they alter these meanings as they move into recovery.[2] Using the paradigm of symbolic interactionism coupled with a feminist perspective, I consider how participants make meaning of activities, actions, and interactions with themselves and others as they become addicts and, later, recovering addicts. Thus, this study demonstrates how, through social action around alcohol and/or drugs, participants' descriptions of how they feel about themselves, about substances, and about others shift and change over time.

How to Study Women's Addiction and Recovery Processes

> In order to be better prepared to provide assistance to women who seek help [for their addiction], it is necessary to know how women extract themselves from problem situations.[3]

Research has revealed that addiction and recovery processes present women with challenges that differ from those confronted by men.[4] Gender differences exist with regard to alcohol and degree of drug use and associated behaviors,[5] as well as to rates of use for various drugs, biological impacts, risk factors, nature of substance use problems, and recommended responses.[6]

Feminist scholars working within a symbolic interactionist paradigm argue for an approach that views the social world through the prism of gender as it intersects with other hierarchies and social forms. Theorizing through a feminist approach works "to make gender visible in social phenomena, asking if, how, and why social processes, standards, and opportunities differ systematically for women and men."[7] Such an approach also recognizes that gender inequality is inextricably entwined with other systems of inequity. Using gender as a lens implies two seemingly contradictory tasks: It means unpacking the taken-for-granted assumptions about gender that pervade sociological research and social life more generally, while at the same time showing just how central assumptions about gender continue to be in the organization of the social world, regardless of their empirical reality.[8]

Using a feminist approach, I draw in concepts of symbolic interactionism to frame my understanding of rural Appalachian women's experiences with addiction and their struggles to recover. Within this framework, the interview process yielded qualitative data that relate to women's perceptions of these experiences. Qualitative research involves a dialectical process of going back and forth between theory, data, and concepts.[9] This approach forces the researcher to confront the methodological implications of what has long been an interactionist maxim but now has become a feminist research tenet: the participants' experiences provide the empirical starting point from which the subjective may be linked to social organization. Thus, I place addiction and recovery at the center of my analysis rather than treating them as dependent variables or using them primarily to support or challenge preexisting sociological or political theories about women's lives.[10] In order to understand social phenomena, the researcher must discover actors' perceptions and interpretations of reality and the ways in which they relate to their behaviors.[11]

A feminist perspective is concerned with equality, empowerment, and social change of both women and men, as well as the elimination of the devaluation and distortion of women's experiences.[12] A feminist approach within the symbolic interactionist paradigm enables me to identify ways in which norms, roles, institutions, and internalized expectations limit women's behaviors. A feminist approach also enables me to demonstrate how women's personal control operates even within the constraints of a relative lack of power.[13] Feminism also takes in alternative viewpoints on the issue of women's addiction and recovery processes, thus providing a broader interpretation of these issues as they relate to women's lives.[14]

Feminism entails "an approach to knowledge that places women at the center of an intellectual analysis and critique of androcentric/phallocentric systems of knowledge."[15] The central objectives of this revisioning of women's lives aim at recapturing, recreating, and revaluing women's knowledge. Women's lives too often have been theorized from a male perspective, meaning that a male standpoint has been represented as universal and that the resulting explanations of women's lives have not corresponded with women's understandings.[16] Feminist scholars attempt to rectify the distortion and invisibility of women's knowledge through historical recovery and contemporary investigation[17] and to replace negative cultural images of women with visions that reaffirm women's strength, capability, and intelligence.

A symbolic interactionist approach considers the ways in which women make sense of their experiences and the impacts of various factors on their lives as they process both addiction and recovery. Three basic assumptions underpin the symbolic interaction paradigm: (1) people act toward things based on the meanings these things have for them; (2) meanings arise out of social interaction; and (3) meanings are modified through an interpretive process that involves self-reflective individuals symbolically interacting with one another.[18]

Symbolic interactionists emphasize human action—or agency—and intersubjectivity and interpretation. Symbolic interactionists see reality as dynamic, meanings as linked to social action and perspectives, and knowledge as an instrumental force that enables people to solve problems.[19] The philosophical underpinnings of a symbolic interactionist viewpoint regard the following as worthy of study: the nature of human action, the makeup of society, the relationship between society and the individual, the importance of the social act, and the appropriateness of "naturalistic" methods for studying human conduct.[20]

I believe that people create the worlds of experience in which they live. Individuals interpret the events and actions that make up their lives based on past experiences and current meanings derived from social interaction. This perspective relies on the assumption that the individual is the final authority in subjective experiences.[21] Therefore, the analyst's task is to understand both these subjective meanings and the larger social context simultaneously. I draw upon Blumer's[22] work in symbolic interactionism, along with concepts of self and reflexivity, combined with more recent work on identity and self-change in this study. Within this framework, I argue that a central feature of women's addiction and recovery lies in their symbolic and interactional relationship with alcohol and/or drugs. The crucial importance of social context, complexity, and diversity of perspectives has become an integral part of feminist theory. In current research, there is a renewed interest in feminist work as a way of understanding the connections between sociopolitical phenomena and personal experiences and there is a renewed respect for the complexity of experiences and change.[23]

Drawing on interdisciplinary works from a wide array of scholars in sociology, psychology, theory, narratology, addiction, and recovery, feminists working within a symbolic interaction paradigm stress an interdisciplinary and multidisciplinary approach, enriching understanding of how women process their addiction and recovery changes. I attempt to continue this understanding through a documentation of twenty-five rural Appalachian women's voices as they experience such processes in this study.

The Problem and Significance of Women's Addiction

Alcohol and drug use continues to afflict both Canadian and American society to a great extent,[24] resulting in serious consequences for those afflicted and for their families.[25] For example, in the United States, 52 million women ages twelve and older reported using an illicit drug at some point in their lives.[26] Among pregnant women aged fifteen to forty-four, 4 percent reported using illicit drugs while pregnant.[27] Approximately 38 percent of female high school students reported using marijuana, and of the 22,000 persons who died of drug-induced causes in 2001, 34 percent were female.[28]

Of the 670,000 individuals admitted to emergency departments nationwide in the United States due to drug use, some 308,000 were women, a 22 percent increase from 1995.[29] Women also accounted for 30 percent of the nationwide admissions to all forms of treatment during 2002.[30] Additional data show that more than half of treatment admissions for sedatives in 2002 involved women.[31]

In 2001, 17,000 females were arrested for drug offense charges.[32] In the United States, women accounted for 8 percent of all federal prisoners serving time for drug offenses.[33] A median of 68 percent of adult female arrestees tested positive for either cocaine, marijuana, methamphetamine, opiates, or PCP during 2003. Overall, between 1995 and 2001, drug offenses accounted for 12 percent of the total prison population growth among female inmates.[34] Nearly one in three women serving time in state prisons said they had committed the offense that brought them to prison in order to obtain money to support their need for drugs.[35]

Of the approximately 40,000 new HIV infections that occur each year in the United States, about 30 percent occur among women.[36] From 1985 to 2002, the proportion of adult and adolescent AIDS cases in the United States reported in women increased from 7 percent to 26 percent.[37] Among teenage women ages thirteen to nineteen, the cumulative number of AIDS cases multiplied more than sixteen times between 1989 and 1997; for women ages twenty to twenty-four, the number multiplied more than nine times during that period. Injection drug use accounted for 28 percent and 14 percent of cases in women in these age groups respectively. Women constitute the fastest-growing group of new HIV cases in the United States.[38] In the state where this study took place, women now make up 8 percent of all reported AIDS cases.[39] Overall, the direct and indirect costs of drug use totaled more than $294 billion (U.S. dollars) in the United States in 2001.[40]

Drug use among Canadian women continues to be a serious issue as well.[41] In a 2002 Canadian Community Epidemiology Network on Drug Use (CCENDU) national report, the percentage of female drinkers increased in Canada, most pronouncedly among twenty- to twenty-four-year-olds. Among Canadian women who were pregnant, 17 to 25 percent reported drinking alcohol during pregnancy. A larger proportion of women than men (23 percent versus 17 percent) reported using at least one mood-altering prescription drug, although, in the general population, women are half as likely as men to be current users of cannabis or any other illegal drug. Women are less likely than men to report legal problems but are more likely to report harm to home life as a result of their substance use.[42]

In Canada, of the 18,124 cumulative AIDS cases in adults, 7.9 percent occurred among women. The proportion of AIDS cases among women (relative to all reported AIDS cases in adults for which gender and age are known) has increased over time from 5.6 percent before 1992 to 8.3 percent in 1995 and peaked at 16.4 percent in 1999. In 2001, the proportion of AIDS cases among women remained at 16 percent.[43]

Annual productivity losses in Canada due to substance use have been estimated at $4.1 billion (Canadian dollars) for alcohol and $823.1 million for illicit drugs.[44] Substance use cost more than $18.4 billion to the Canadian economy in 1992, representing 2.7 percent of the gross national product in that year.[45] Substance use among women is a major health, legal, economic, and social issue in North America.[46] Alcohol and/or drug use among women has serious implications both for society and for women struggling with their addictions. Issues of concern include the increase in HIV/AIDS among women in both rural and urban areas as a consequence of unsafe sex; family disruptions; impaired performance at work, in some cases resulting in loss of employment; growth in the female population in U.S. prisons; depression; victimization due to disproportionate vulnerability to attack; increased mental and social problems; and physiological risks, such as reproductive problems, physical disabilities, and, finally, death.[47] Furthermore, the use of alcohol and drugs during pregnancy not only affects mothers but also often has a profound and irreversible effect on their fetuses.[48] The cost of alcohol and/or drug use among both rural and urban women is high in both personal and social terms for both the United States and Canada in the twenty-first century.

Men and women face very different challenges in addiction and recovery.[49] Both in the United States and in Canada, addiction policy researchers argue that a full understanding of the problems associated with alcohol and/or drug use among women requires an analysis of the status of women within a feminist theoretical framework.[50] Too often, as Blackwell et al. argue, "the authors of substance abuse literature inappropriately extrapolate from men's experiences in order to understand those of women."[51] A feminist framework favors sound empirical research that seeks to gain an understanding of the daily realties faced by women who use alcohol and/or drugs. Furthermore, "[a] feminist framework rejects the value of research that consists of an extrapolation of research conducted on men, or that is founded on assumptions based on traditional feminine roles."[52]

From a feminist perspective, attempts to treat alcohol and/or drug use problems in women should be directed at the whole woman, "taking into account her history and her life circumstances and not just her substance use."[53] Many feminist scholars are uncomfortable with the medical model, the disease model, and the Alcoholics Anonymous (AA) or twelve-step model.[54] Both Canadian and American feminist scholars[55] favor evaluating the larger sociopolitical context in which women in general and, more specifically, women who seek help for alcohol and/or drug use currently live. Further research should focus on women's individual experiences in addiction and recovery processes in order to provide insights into their individual needs and concerns.

A symbolic interactionist framework coupled with a feminist lens enables me to explore and to understand the daily realities faced by rural Appalachian women formerly addicted to alcohol and/or drugs. This framework offers a critical approach that views alcohol and/or drug use as a "gender-illuminating issue,"[56] an approach that is more sensitive to the needs of rural women as a social group. Ettorre argues that

> [there is a need to] explore the ways in which the experiences of women substance users can be recognized and valued. [One way to begin is to create] a critical framework in which the production of feminist knowledge becomes a real possibility within this field. We need images of women substance users that empower rather than stigmatise or victimize them. [We need to gain] a distinct view of the way "masculinist" ways of thinking can be appropriately challenged in the substance use field.[57]

Women have been largely absent from symbolic interactionist studies on the prevalence and processes of addiction and recovery. There is an absence of research that offers a gender-based analysis of rural Appalachian women's processes of addiction/recovery. This study then brings into play women's agency, women's autonomy, and the centrality of gender, helping to generate a better understanding of rural Appalachian women's lives as they process addiction and recovery experiences.

Feminism and Symbolic Interaction

As a researcher following the principles of feminism within a symbolic interaction lens, I consider how the participating women constructed meaning, used symbols, and determined their courses of action. As Crooks argues:

> Research based on symbolic interactionism reveals the world view of women by seeking to understand the social construction of meaning and action by asking questions about point of view, influences on action, problem-solving strategies, definition of action and situation, effect of past experiences, and, finally, future plans.[58]

In order to provide meaningful, evidence-based care to women, researchers need to attend to women's experiences, their understanding of issues, and the social interactions within which they gain meanings and insights about their situations.[59] Feminism within a symbolic interactionist lens is ideal for investigating "relatively uncharted waters,"[60] that is, when important variables in the addiction and recovery field have yet to be determined.

Denzin[61] explains symbolic interactionism as a study of the intersections of interaction, biography, and social structure in people's lives. To study these intersections, it is important to have an understanding of the basic elements, to recognize the dynamism between elements, and to focus on the struggle to make sense of the self and life experiences. People do not come to know themselves directly, but only through play, social interaction, reflection, and putting themselves in the position of the interacting individual.[62]

Central to one's biography is the self. Blumer[63] viewed the self as a uniquely human attribute developed through a continuous process of social interaction. Through social intercourse with others and within the self, the self is conceptualized and reconceptualized over time.[64] As one becomes an object of one's own action, meaning is derived. Mead[65] argued that one is able to become an object to oneself through the words "I" and "me." "I" is the creative, unpredictable aspect of the self, reactive to the immediate situation. The situation provides the motivation for change and for new understanding. "I" is known only in memory, as one reflects on one's actions. The "me" is the organized set of attitudes of others, which one assumes as part of a social group or society. The "me" is visible as habitual, conventional action and conscious responsibility.[66] Selves may share a common structure, but each self is multilayered, created within unique social and biographical contexts.[67]

A change in one's life, a social crisis, or a loss of some type may create both upheaval and opportunity. Denzin argues that "epiphanic experiences rupture routines and lives and provide radical redefinitions of the self."[68] The "I" reacts creatively to the experience, and the "me" stabilizes the meanings formed and the choices made. In making choices, people point out to themselves those things that have meaning in the situation through a process of inward communication. Interpretation of meanings leads to selection, grouping, and regrouping of meanings within the present situation, and the newly constructed meaning ultimately directs action.[69] As a result, one acts toward oneself and guides oneself in her actions in the situation.[70] The person "is an acting organism who has to forge and direct [a] line of action."[71] As the individual interprets the world in a minded fashion, thinking and action are reformulated in an iterative and expanding way. The reflexive action of "turning back experience upon [one] self" brings the social process into the experience of the individual involved in it.[72] In this way, experiences can be shared with others.

Mead[73] argues that an understanding of human beings is inferred from what they do. Therefore, the guiding question in feminist research should be "What do women do in a given situation?" Examination of thought processes must be a central concern of any investigation of what it is to be human.[74] Charon[75] argues that to comprehend fully, one must observe, partake, and interview. Ritzer[76] identifies three points critical to any study using symbolic interactionism: (1) a focus on the interaction between the actor and the world, (2) a view of the actor and the world as dynamic processes, and (3) the importance of the actor's ability to interpret the social world.

In a feminist analysis of addiction and recovery through a symbolic interactionist lens, a researcher understands what is going on if and only if she or he understands women's beliefs about their social worlds and their experiences and how such experiences shape their worlds. A study of women's experiences in addiction and recovery requires a model that attends to a variety of contextual variables, including women's perceptions, attributions of meaning, relationships, caring responsibilities, and preferences for interaction.

Feminism coupled with symbolic interaction provides a focus for meaningful research into women's experiences as they process their addiction and recovery. In this study, I consider twenty-five rural Appalachian women's personal experiences of their social worlds of addiction and recovery. The following discussion highlights the basic premises of feminism within symbolic interaction as considered throughout this study.

Basic Premises of Feminism and Symbolic Interaction

The following discussion provides an overview of how I use a feminist approach to symbolic interactionism in this study. "Feminist" came into widespread usage in the western world in the 1890s. It emerged as a way to identify individuals who supported an increased public role for women along with women's right to define themselves as autonomous beings. In the intervening years, the definition has expanded and altered to include political, cultural, economic, sexual, racial, and ethical dimensions.[77]

A feminist perspective should be involved in changing society, raising feminist consciousness, and working to reduce gender inequality.[78] Chafetz[79] argues that there are three specific elements that render a theory "feminist":

> (1) Gender comprises a central focus or subject matter of the theory. Feminist theory seeks to understand the gendered nature of virtually all social relations, institutions, and processes.
> (2) Gender relations are viewed as a problem; therefore, feminist theory seeks to understand how gender is related to social inequalities, strain, and contradictions.
> (3) Gender relations are not viewed as either natural or immutable. Rather, the gender-related status quo is viewed as the product of sociocultural and historical forces that have been created—and are constantly recreated—by humans and therefore potentially can be changed by human agency.

Bologh states that "[f]eminist theorizing promises not only to fill the gaps in knowledge about women but to provide an alternative perception of the world that men, because of their (dominant) position, could not possess."[80] Smith[81] argues that feminist research overall should never lose sight of women as actively constructing, as well as interpreting, the social processes and realities that constitute their everyday lives. Smith's view[82] is similar to a symbolic interactionist approach, which insists that "what is going on out there is what the actors say is going on out there" and that such actors are experts about their own world.[83]

Various studies have been conducted on women's ways of knowing and how women perceive themselves to be heard, valued, and respected.[84] "Gaining a voice" arose as a central metaphor of women's experiences and development.[85] Of special importance to research on women's issues are the developmental categories of silences, subjective knowledge, and constructed knowledge.[86] Ways of knowing are important in both feminism and symbolic interaction. Both subjective and constructed knowledge provide the data for study and are key to identifying women's processes and changes in addiction and recovery.

Women's experiences are situated and embedded in a social context and are variously located in society.[87] Smith argues that "[a] sociology for women preserves the presence of subjects as knowers and as actors."[88] We start, therefore, with women's experiences; we begin in the particularities of women's actual everyday worlds. We start from the "standpoint of women"[89] and from where we are in the everyday world. We start "talking about a world that actually happens and can be observed."[90] Feminism coupled with symbolic interaction is one means of giving women a voice because it assists in "continually bringing into being as it is and as it is becoming, in the daily practices of actual individuals."[91]

Garfinkel[92] argues that in doing sociology every reference to the real world is a reference to the organized activities of everyday life. In any given context of action, the social arises in how individuals enter actual courses of action coordinating with others, with objects, and with an environment that is already socially organized and that is becoming organized again as they act.[93] Therefore, a feminist social inquiry within a symbolic interactionist framework proposes a method of inquiry that relies on women's experiences and existences in common, continually created and recreated in human activities.[94]

Furthermore, feminist theories often are explicitly political in inspiration and in their advocacy for social change.[95] As Chafetz argues, "The politics of feminist theories are only more self-conscious and explicit, not more intrusive or biasing, than those of most other theories."[96] In this study, I attempt to explicate rural Appalachian women's stories of their addiction and recovery experiences, thereby suggesting a feminist theory within the paradigm of symbolic interactionism for such processes in these women's lives.

Outline of the Chapters

Chapter 1 discusses the research methodology, including the background and context of the study. Chapter 2 explores women's preaddicted selves, highlighting their feelings and experiences of their individual and social identities in what I term *The Preexperimental Self* and *The Experimental Self* phases, before alcohol and/or drug use becomes the main focus of their lives.

Chapter 3, *The Addicted Self* phase, focuses on participants' addicted selves, highlighting the pleasure and fun they derive from use of substances, along with other social experiences women undergo while immersed in alcohol and/or drug culture. Chapter 3 also introduces women's experiences of "disgusted selves," which begin to appear as they rethink alcohol and/or drug use. Women begin to experience and realize that substances no longer work for them.

Chapter 4 highlights important factors implicit in women's experiences as they leave addiction: How they begin recovery processes through the creation of what I call *The Recovering Self* phase, their awareness of the need for change, the strategies they use to validate their emergent "strategic selves" and, finally, how they continue to generate "stable selves" as they continue abstinence in their lives.

Chapter 5 concludes the study and analyzes implications for understanding rural Appalachian women and their meanings toward their addiction and recovery processes.

Notes

1. U. Duongsaa, "Women, Gender and Drugs" (speech presented to UNDP panel discussion on Drugs and Development at the United Nations General Assembly Special Session on Drugs, New York, June 1998), 1.

2. N. Campbell, *Gender, Drug Policy, and Social Justice: Using Women* (New York: Routledge, 2000); N. Van Den Bergh, "Having Bitten the Apple: A Feminist Perspective on Addictions," in *Feminist Perspectives on Addiction*, ed. N. Van Den Bergh (New York: Springer, 1991), 3–30.

3. J. Blackwell, W. E. Thurston, and K. Graham, "Women's Use of Alcohol, Tobacco and Other Drugs in Canada," in *Canadian Women and Substance Use: Overview and Policy Implications*, ed. M. Adrian, C. Lundy, and M. Eliany (Toronto, Ontario: Addiction Research Foundation, 1996), 228–46.

4. A. A. Abbot, "Substance Use and the Feminist Perspective," in *Feminist Practice in the 21st Century*, ed. N. Van Den Bergh (Washington, DC: National Association of Social Workers Press, 1995), 258–78; Campbell, *Gender, Drug Policy, and Social Justice;* Van Den Bergh, "Having Bitten the Apple," 3–30.

5. C. Grella and V. Joshi, "Gender Differences in Drug Treatment Careers among Clients in the National Drug Use Treatment Outcome Study," *American Journal of Drug and Alcohol Use* 25 (1999): 385.

6. C. A. Dell and K. Garabedian, *Canadian Community Epidemiology Network on Drug Use: 2002 National Report* (Ottawa, Ontario: Canadian Center on Substance Use, 2003).

7. M. M. Ferree, J. Lorder, and B. B. Heiss, *Revisioning Gender* (Thousand Oaks, CA: Sage, 1999), xiii.

8. Ferree, Lorder, and Heiss, *Revisioning Gender*, xiii.

9. B. Glaser and A. Strauss, *The Discovery of Grounded Theory: Strategies for Qualitative Research* (Chicago: Aldine, 1967).

10. M. McMahon, *Engendering Motherhood: Identity and Self-Transformation in Women's Lives* (New York: Guilford, 1995).

11. H. Schwartz and J. Jacobs, *Qualitative Sociology: A Method to the Madness* (New York: Macmillan, 1979).

12. S. Reinharz, *Feminist Methods in Social Research* (New York: Oxford University Press, 1992).

13. A. Stewart, "Toward a Feminist Strategy for Studying Women's Lives," in *Women Creating Lives: Identities, Resilience, and Resistance*, ed. C. Franz and A. Stewart (Boulder, CO: Westview, 1994), 11–35.

14. Reinharz, *Feminist Methods in Social Research.*

15. N. Mandell, introduction to *Feminist Issues: Race, Class, and Sexuality,* ed. N. Mandell (Scarborough, Ontario: Prentice Hall Canada, 1995), vii–viii.

16. D. Smith, *The Everyday World as Problematic: A Feminist Sociology* (Toronto, Ontario: University of Toronto Press, 1987).

17. Mandell, introduction, vii–viii.

18. H. Blumer, *Symbolic Interactionism: Perspective and Method* (Englewood Cliffs, NJ: Prentice Hall, 1969).

19. K. D. Sandstrom, D. Martin, and G. Fine, *Symbols, Selves, and Social Reality: A Symbolic Interactionist Approach to Social Psychology and Sociology* (Los Angeles: Roxbury, 2003), 15.

20. Sandstrom, Martin, and Fine, *Symbols, Selves, and Social Reality,* 15.

21. N. Denzin, *Symbolic Interactionism and Cultural Studies: The Politics of Interpretation* (Oxford: Blackwell, 1992).

22. Blumer, *Symbolic Interactionism.*

23. E. Kaschak, *Engendered Lives: A New Psychology of Women's Experiences* (New York: Basic Books, 1992).

24. M. Adrian, C. Lundy, and M. Eliany, eds., *Canadian Women and Substance Use: Overview and Policy Implications* (Toronto, Ontario: Addiction Research Foundation, 1996).

25. Abbott, "Substance Use and the Feminist Perspective," 258–78.

26. Substance Abuse and Mental Health Services Administration (SAMHSA), *Results from the 2003 National Survey on Drug Use and Health* (Washington, DC: Department of Health and Human Services, 2004).

27. SAMHSA, *Results from the 2003 National Survey.*

28. Centers for Disease Control (CDC), *Youth Risk Behavior Surveillance, United States, 2003* 53 (2004): 1–96.

29. Centers for Disease Control, *HIV and AIDS—United States, 1981–2001* 50 (2001): 430–34.

30. SAMHSA, *Results from the 2003 National Survey.*

31. SAMHSA, *Results from the 2003 National Survey.*

32. Bureau of Justice Statistics (BJS), *Compendium of Federal Justice Statistics,* 2003.

33. BJS, *Compendium of Federal Justice Statistics,* 2003.

34. BJS, *Compendium of Federal Justice Statistics,* 2003.

35. BJS, *Women Offenders,* http://www.ojp.usdoj.gov/bjs/ (6 Feb. 2007).

36. CDC, *HIV/AIDS Surveillance Report* 9 (2001).

37. CDC, *HIV/AIDS Surveillance Report;* SAMHSA, *Results from the 2003 National Survey.*

38. CDC, *HIV/AIDS Surveillance Report,* 2001; SAMHSA, *Results from the 2003 National Survey.*

39. T. Tatum, "Rural Women's Recovery Program and Women's Outreach," *Substance Abuse and Mental Health Services Administration,* http://www.treatment.org/TAPS/TAP17/tap17rural.html (16 May 2006).

40. Office of National Drug Policy, *The Escalating Costs of Drug Abuse in the U.S., 1992–2002* (Washington, DC: Office of National Drug Control Policy, 2001).

41. Adrian, Lundy, and Eliany, *Canadian Women and Substance Use.*

42. Dell and Garabedian, *Canadian Community Epidemiology Network on Drug Use.*

43. Centre for Infectious Disease Prevention and Control, Health Canada, *National HIV Prevalence and Incidence Estimates for 1999: No Evidence of a Decline in Overall Incidence* (Ottawa, Ontario: Public Health Agency of Canada, 2003).

44. Canadian Centre on Substance Abuse (CCSA), *CCSA Canadian Profile*

http://www.ccsa.ca/index.asp (19 November 2004).

45. CCSA, *CCSA Canadian Profile.*

46. Adrian, Lundy, and Eliany, *Canadian Women and Substance Use;* Campbell, *Gender, Drug Policy, and Social Justice;* E. Goode, *Drugs in American Society,* fifth ed. (Boston: McGraw-Hill, 1999).

47. Abbot, "Substance Use and the Feminist Perspective," 258–78.

48. Abbot, "Substance Use and the Feminist Perspective," 258–78.

49. Abbot, "Substance Use and The Feminist Perspective," 258–78; Adrian, Lundy, and Eliany, *Canadian Women and Substance Use;* Campbell, *Gender, Drug Policy, and Social Justice;* E. Ettorre, *Women and Substance Use* (London: Macmillan, 1992); Goode, *Drugs in American Society;* M. Plant, *Women and Alcohol: Contemporary and Historical Perspectives* (London: Free Association Books, 1997); Van Den Bergh, "Having Bitten the Apple," 3–30.

50. Blackwell, Thurston, and Graham, "Women's Use of Alcohol, Tobacco and Other Drugs in Canada"; Campbell, *Gender, Drug Policy, and Social Justice;* Ettorre, *Women and Substance Use,* 30.

51. Blackwell, Thurston, and Graham, "Women's Use of Alcohol, Tobacco and Other Drugs in Canada," 30.

52. Blackwell, Thurston, and Graham, "Women's Use of Alcohol, Tobacco and Other Drugs in Canada," 231.

53. Blackwell, Thurston, and Graham, "Women's Use of Alcohol, Tobacco and Other Drugs in Canada," 240.

54. Ettorre, *Women and Substance Use.*

55. Blackwell, Thurston, and Graham, "Women's Use of Alcohol, Tobacco and Other Drugs in Canada"; Campbell, *Gender, Drug Policy, and Social Justice;* Ettorre, *Women and Substance Use,* 228–46.

56. Ettorre, *Women and Substance Use,* 11.

57. Ettorre, *Women and Substance Use,* 16.

58. D. Crooks, "The Importance of Symbolic Interaction in Grounded Theory Research on Women's Health," *Health Care for Women's International* 22 (2001): 20.

59. Crooks, "Importance of Symbolic Interaction," 12.

60. Crooks, "Importance of Symbolic Interaction," 12.

61. Denzin, *Symbolic Interactionism and Cultural Studies,* 26.

62. Crooks, "Importance of Symbolic Interaction," 20.

63. Blumer, *Symbolic Interactionism,* 55.

64. Blumer, *Symbolic Interactionism,* 55.

65. G. H. Mead, *Mind, Self and Society from the Standpoint of a Social Behaviorist,* ed. C. Morris (Chicago: University of Chicago Press, 1934).

66. Mead, *Mind, Self and Society.*

67. Crooks, "Importance of Symbolic Interaction," 20.

68. Denzin, *Symbolic Interactionism,* 26.

69. Crooks, "Importance of Symbolic Interaction," 20

70. Blumer, *Symbolic Interactionism,* 55.

71. Blumer, *Symbolic Interactionism,* 55.

72. Mead, *Mind, Self and Society from the Standpoint of a Social Behaviorist Mind,* 134.

73. Mead, *Mind, Self and Society from the Standpoint of a Social Behaviorist Mind,* 134.

74. Crooks, "Importance of Symbolic Interaction," 20.

75. J. Charon, *Symbolic Interactionism: An Introduction, an Interpretation, an Integration,* seventh ed. (Upper Saddle River, NJ: Prentice Hall, 2001).

76. G. Ritzer, *Contemporary Sociological Theory,* third ed. (New York: McGraw-

Hill, 1992).

77. P. Elliott and N. Mandell, "Feminist Theories," in *Feminist Issues: Race, Class, and Sexuality,* ed. N. Mandell (Scarborough, Ontario: Prentice Hall Canada, 1995), 3–31.

78. J. S. Chafetz, *Feminist Sociology: An Overview of Contemporary Theories* (Itasca, IL: F. E. Peacock Publishers, 1988).

79. Chafetz, *Feminist Sociology.*

80. R. W. Bologh, "Feminist Social Theorizing and Moral Reasoning on Difference and Dialectic," in *Sociological Theory,* ed. R. Collins (San Francisco: Jossey-Bass, 1984), 382.

81. D. Smith, *The Everyday World as Problematic: A Feminist Sociology* (Toronto, Ontario: University of Toronto Press, 1987), 105.

82. Smith, *Everyday World as Problematic,* 105.

83. R. Lentin, "I'll Be a Post-Feminist in Post-Patriarchy: Reflexivity Is a Feminist Issue," http://www.iol.ie/~mazzoldi/toolsforchange/postmet/feminist.html (16 November 2004).

84. L. Code, *What Can She Know? Feminist Theory and the Construction of Knowledge* (Ithaca, NY: Cornell University Press, 1991); C. Gilligan, *In a Different Voice: Psychological Theory and Women's Development* (Cambridge, MA: Harvard University Press, 1993); Smith, *Everyday World as Problematic.*

85. Crooks, "Importance of Symbolic Interaction," 15.

86. Code, *What Can She Know?;* Crooks, "Importance of Symbolic Interaction," 15.

87. Smith, *Everyday World as Problematic,* 105.

88. Smith, *Everyday World as Problematic,* 105.

89. Smith, *Everyday World as Problematic,* 122.

90. Smith, *Everyday World as Problematic,* 123.

91. Smith, *Everyday World as Problematic,* 125.

92. H. Garfinkel, *Studies in Ethnomethodology* (Englewood Cliffs, NJ: Prentice Hall, 1967).

93. Smith, *Everyday World as Problematic,* 125.

94. G. H. Mead, *The Philosophy of the Act* (Chicago: University of Chicago Press, 1938); Smith, *Everyday World as Problematic,* 125.

95. Chafetz, *Feminist Sociology;* Elliott and Mandell, "Feminist Theories," 3–31.

96. Chafetz, *Feminist Sociology,* 6.

Chapter 1

Methodology

Introduction

> In many qualitative studies, the real interest is in how participants make sense of what has happened, and how this perspective informs their actions, rather than determining precisely what they did.[1]

I employed a qualitative feminist research methodology in this study. As Comack[2] argues, one of the goals of feminism is to produce knowledge that is women-centered; feminists want women's voices and experiences to be heard. Positivistic research generally does not call for the subjective[3] within the research design, but, in many cases, it views men's knowledge as universal and that of others contingent.[4]

Inquiry into women's experiences of addiction and recovery processes is well suited to the symbolic interactionist paradigm. Blumer[5] argues that understanding the process of social action consists of exploring the processes by which several individuals, or "selves," mutually adjust various lines of action on the basis of their ongoing interpretations of the world. In order to do this, one must necessarily get into what is called the "reality reconstruction business."[6] Blumer states:

> On the methodological or research side the study of action would have to be made from the position of the actor. Since action is forged by the actor out of what [she] perceives, interprets, and judges, one would have to see the operating situation as the actor sees it, perceive objects as the actor perceives them, ascertain their meaning in terms of the meanings they have for the actor, and follow the actor's line of conduct as the actor organizes it—in short, one would have to take the role of the actor and see [her] world from [her] standpoint.[7]

The principal tool is observation, often divided into two types: (1) exploration and (2) inspection.[8] Feminist qualitative research provides a link to the symbolic interactionist approach whereby participants provide the researcher with a valuable reflection of their own realities, definitions, and a consideration that highlights their agencies and praxis within their experiences. Therefore, this feminist qualitative study is grounded in the understanding of a feminist social-structural and individual critique of participants' positions within both addiction and recovery processes.

Feminist theories recognize that much past research is based on patriarchal ideological conditioning.[9] Language used by male authors in texts, science journals, reports, and other studies is male-oriented and generally revolves around male-centered ideas.[10] Such research rarely uncovers much about the content and texture of a person's life. Amid factorial analyses and mean T-scores, the essence of experience—feelings, thoughts, turning points—tends to get lost. The best way to recover that experience is to give women the opportunity to talk about themselves, freely and at length.[11] Anderson and Jack[12] argue that the interview is a critical tool for developing new frameworks and theories based on women's lives and women's formulations. Interviewers who validate women by using women's communication are midwives for women's words.[13]

Harding maintains that "never was what counts as general social knowledge generated by asking questions from the perspectives of women's lives."[14] Scholarship on women, for the most part, has not contributed to the construction of women's lives, either through women's voices, women's writings, or through women's activism.[15] Some theories simply ignore women,[16] and some assume that women's lives are like men's.[17]

Several scholars[18] have provided rich discussion concerning women's lives, but much work still needs to be done. We know little about the development of self changes among former rural women addicts. We know little about how and why women manage to circumvent the labels we have been given, as men's standpoint is usually represented as universal.[19] We know little about how women become "knowers" when the "stereotypes construct women as 'generalized' objects of knowledge that are often sharply discontinuous from women's self-conceptions and self-understandings."[20]

In carrying out this study, I follow a qualitative feminist approach by including rural women's experiences as they voiced them. Participants are not objects of study, but subjects of critical importance. My method of research consists of an existential sociology, which can be described as "the study of human experience-in-the-world in all its forms."[21] Such methods recognize feelings, not just ideas about observing, describing, and analyzing one's own inner experiences and reflections. Reinharz has labeled this approach "experiential analysis"[22] in order to distinguish it from existentialism and phenomenology, to avoid connotations of rigidity connected to a specified philosophical school, and to create a term that is descriptive of a specific activity that provides an analysis of experience. Research that is experientially based provides a richer database with greater detail.[23] This, in turn, leads to greater descriptive power in the resultant analysis.

Semi-structured or unstructured interviewing[24] is a qualitative data-gathering technique commonly used in feminist work. As Graham states, "The use of semi-structured interviews has become the principal means by which feminists have sought to achieve the active involvement of their respondents in the construction of data about their lives."[25] I use this method because it makes possible free interaction between the women and myself and maximizes the discovery and description of their lives. Such interviewing allows the women to bring out their ideas, thoughts, and memories in their own words rather than in my words.

As Anderson and Jack argue, "If our questions are general enough, women will be able to reflect upon their experience and choose for themselves which experiences and feelings are central to their sense of their past."[26] For example, when I asked participants to tell me about their lives before their addiction began, they told me about their lives as young girls, including self-images, relationships, education, and often moral dilemmas, thus enhancing my initial research questions. Enabling my participants to expand on semi-structured questions makes it possible for them to respond in their own terms to experiences that are important to them. The semi-structured interview format gives participants considerable freedom to share whatever information they feel is most important, including issues that might not be considered by the interviewer.[27] The use of loosely structured interview questions allows the researcher to adjust the research questions as more data comes to light. This reflective process leads to a deeper understanding of the issues and honors the individuality of each participant.

The central concern of my research is a context-specific interpretive analysis[28] whereby I look for meanings from women themselves as they relate stories of addiction and recovery. The theoretical challenge of this work is to analyze rural women's experiences in a way that captures agency and, at the same time, recognizes the persistence of shared patterns of meanings that emerge from women's experiences and actions.[29] In the qualitative, interpretive analysis, the objective is to find patterns within rural women's lives as they proceed through experiences that lead to their addiction and, later, to their recovery. Symbolic interactionism focuses on the nature of social interactions, the dynamic and social activities taking place among actors.[30] Within this perspective, more active images of participants are forthcoming; women are constantly undergoing changes in their interactions. The interplay of complex factors that impinge on recovered women's lives cannot be analyzed apart from the larger contexts in which women live or their resultant experiences. Therefore, I ground the conceptualizations and arguments that participants provide and attempt to tell their stories, as much as possible, from their points of view[31] as they act and react within processes of addiction and recovery. Facts and interpretations shape one another; they constitute a continuum rather than a dichotomy.[32]

This study looks for reasons that clarify the meanings of recovered women's behavior through their narratives, making explicit their place in society in a broader feminist and symbolic interactionist analysis. Stivers states that

> [t]he sense of self is an essentially narrative phenomenon; people conceive of themselves in terms of stories about their actions in the world, using them to make sense of the temporal flow of their lives.

> We find identity and meaning as a result of the stories we tell about ourselves or that others tell about us. Therefore, a narrative approach to self-understanding is not a distortion of reality but a confirmation of it.[33]

Within the qualitative method of this study, I used rural women's contextual knowledge gained through stories shared in the interviews. Stivers[34] argues that feminist interest in personal narrative is grounded on the claim that the subject's understanding of her life is inherently valid and that individual interpretations constitute a societal change process. She further elaborates that there is room in critical social science for personal narratives because they meld life and theory, providing the grounding for an impulse toward social change that acknowledges the fundamental authenticity of an interpretation based on direct experience.[35] Personal narratives help feminist social scientists center themselves in knowledge development and in the widening of the feminist knowledge community.

In this study, I give participants the opportunity to make their voices and experiences known and to contribute to the ongoing community of knowledge development within feminist work through my subsequent interpretation and analysis of these women's narratives. The narrative shapes the interpretation the participant gives of the events of her life, and this becomes the point of that life.[36]

A methodology that encompasses symbolic interactionism and feminist-centered research has two approaches: first, to give rise to a different definition of women's experiences as social actors and, second, to investigate subjective aspects of such experiences.[37] Therefore, this study has two purposes. The first is to describe, from participants' perspectives, how twenty-five rural Appalachian women became addicted to alcohol and/or drugs and how they discontinued their use of such substances through recovery processes. The second is to analyze the processes that enabled these women to become addicted and to recover from addictions.

In this study, I draw on six feminist strategies that Stewart[38] suggests are useful for studying women's lives. I argue that these feminist strategies help scholars render women's lives with respect for agency, complexity, and the constraints under which women operate.[39]

The following strategies serve as guidelines for this study as I consider the many facets of rural Appalachian women's lives in terms of addiction and recovery processes:

(1) Look for what has been left out. As Stewart[40] suggests, this strategy entails a consideration of what has been left out, overlooked, and unnoticed in scientific research, in this case, individual rural Appalachian women's lives and experiences that have not been deemed sufficiently important in recovery and addiction research.[41]

(2) Analyze your own role or position as it affects your understanding and the research process. This particular strategy involves reflexivity on the part of the researcher, who must consider consciously and systematically the ways in which her or his demographic and ideological characteristics may affect the work. For example, before entering York University in Toronto, Canada, to pur-

sue my PhD, I worked in the community for three years with women who were recovering from their use of alcohol and/or drugs.[42] These experiences helped me to cultivate a sensitivity to women I interviewed for this study.

(3) Identify women's agency in the midst of social constraint. Stewart[43] suggests that within the context of relative powerlessness, women make choices and resist oppression. She further argues that recognizing agency is sometimes complicated and difficult; but assuming that it is there can help. This study, therefore, recognizes and documents agency through women's experiences, even if they do not perceive it themselves.

(4) Use the concept of gender as an analytical tool. In studying women's lives, one must always inquire into an understanding of how gender affects their lives. Because feminist theory is grounded in women's lives and analyzes the role and meaning of gender in those lives and in society, women's personal narratives are essential documents for feminist research.[44] This study takes into consideration how recovering women perceive the ways in which gender affects their lives.

(5) Explore the precise ways in which gender defines power relationships and in which power relationships are gendered. My analysis focuses on whether women participants experience a sense of powerlessness, strain, or marginality in specific relationships and what meanings these have for them.

(6) Avoid the search for a unified or a coherent self or voice. My analysis considers rural women's many and varied voices and documents the inconsistencies and complexities of participants' life experiences. Stewart[45] suggests that researchers need to notice the many different voices of women for the same reason that it is important to notice that women have something to say at all: "Silencing voices always leaves us without knowledge. Listening will leave us with more."[46] In this study, I attempt to do just that.

Feminism, as a model of analysis, is the antithesis of a patriarchal, capitalist perspective. It is a liberation philosophy promoting both nurture of the self and concern with collective well-being.[47] Van Den Bergh argues that "[t]he feminist approach includes working collaboratively, collectively and cooperatively; valuing personal experiences; encouraging growth and development; caring for others, building supportive relationships as well as believing in the interconnectedness of people and events."[48]

In summary, a feminist qualitative research approach enables the researcher to understand the meanings that participants attach to events, situations, and actions, including the accounts that women give of their lives and their experiences. Participants' meanings include cognition, affect, and intentions that incorporate their perspectives.[49] In other words, I am interested in how participants make sense of their addiction and recovery and how these understandings influence their behaviors. This emphasis on understanding processes by which events and actions take place is another strength of the qualitative approach. Such "process theory"[50] deals with events and the various processes that connect them; it is based on an analysis of the causal processes by which some events influence others. Of primary interest in this study are participants' definitions of addiction and recovery and their interpretations of how they make meanings of such experiences. Therefore, the approach and methodology used throughout this study comprises both the symbolic interactionist perspective and feminist qualitative work.

Background and Context of the Study

As I previously stated, much of what is known about rural Appalachian women's experiences in the recovery field fails to address how they think, how they organize ideas, and what is meaningful to them.[51] Although symbolic interactionists argue that individuals have many selves created by social interactions, the "multifocal nature of womanhood"[52] has received little attention. Crooks argues that

> [r]esearch based on symbolic interactionism reveals the world view of women by seeking to understand the social construction of meaning and action by asking questions about point of view, influences on action, problem-solving strategies, definition of action and situation, effect of past experiences, and, finally, future plans.[53]

Research has revealed that addiction and recovery processes present challenges to women that differ from those confronted by men.[54] Gender differences exist with regard to alcohol and degree of drug use and associated behaviors,[55] as well as to rates of use for various drugs, biological impacts, risk factors, nature of substance use problems, and recommended responses.[56] Much of the literature generates stereotypical images of women who use alcohol and/or drugs, distorting their experiences and minimizing their challenges.[57] So, too, concerns about women and their use of such substances has had an intensely moral tone around essentially moral issues: the supposed effects of alcohol and other drug use on women's "maternal instincts," their ability to care for children and partners, their sexualities, and the destruction of their "female purity."[58] Moreover, female users have generally been considered more pathological than male users.[59]

Various authors have researched the recovery process,[60] but these studies have primarily involved male addicts. However, three significant studies have considered women's lives through a symbolic interactionist lens: one on urban women addicted to heroin,[61] and one on urban pregnant women using drugs.[62] The third important study is Raine's[63] work in England on urban women's perspectives on alcohol use and the centrality of gender in their lives.

There are a growing number of studies that consider women's patterns of alcohol and/or drug use.[64] Such studies examine why women turn to and, ultimately, leave their use of substances, but there is no research on how rural Appalachian women experience or "make meaning" of such processes for themselves. How rural Appalachian women experience addiction and modify their recovery processes is absent from the literature.

As participants attempt to process their recovery from use of alcohol and/or drugs, I argue that they use strategies that allowed for meaningful action through three self-changing processes: (1) *The Preaddicted Self*, (2) *The Addicted Self*, and (3) *The Recovering Self*. These topics are not the only ones I heard in my research. They by no means exhaust the possibilities. I have chosen to treat these three in depth because they represent topics that I heard repeatedly. In other words, they illustrate the ways in which addiction and recovery become part of the resources that shape participants' stories and that, consequently, shape their selves.[65]

"Strategy," as used in this study, is defined as a process of creating new social environments and new courses of action, a process of forging new social bonds and social structures in order to help participants depart from previous habits of using alcohol and/or drugs. Strategies are common among former addicts,[66] and in this study such strategies reflected the conscious activities in which participants engaged as they broke away from addiction and which were necessary components in their recovery. How do the participants accomplish these things? What resources do they manage to acquire and make use of in their efforts? What strategies do they develop? And how do they reassert a sense of positive selves? Finally, how successful are these strategies in enabling them to manage and/or transcend their previous self-images? These are the questions I address in the following pages. In the process, I hope to shed light on both the women as strategic actors and the social dimension that helped them reassert their sense of selves. I describe a range of strategies in each category.

Central Appalachia, where this study took place, includes the defined geographic area of West Virginia as well as parts of Kentucky, Tennessee, Virginia, and Ohio, where a higher proportion of the almost entirely white (93.5 percent), largely rural population is poor. Approximately 65 percent of Appalachian counties are rural: 42 percent of the region's residents live in these rural counties. Rates of poverty and unemployment are well known. Rural populations in the United States tend to be poorer and sicker than the overall population, and rural women are no exception. In addition, rural people have lower rates of employer-sponsored insurance coverage, lower rates of insurance overall, and less access to specialist care. In many rural areas, primary care services may be difficult to access because of a lack of providers, barriers due to geographic distance or terrain, or a lack of transportation.[67]

Half of the state residents have an income of under $20,000, and half are unemployed or homemakers.[68] Appalachia today is a region of contrasts: tradition versus progress, stability versus growth, regional markets versus international markets, agriculture versus industry, and family versus the individual. Much of Appalachia remains a poverty-stricken, economically depressed, and underserved area.[69]This region has traditionally experienced higher poverty rates, lower education levels, and limited access to health care as compared to the nation as a whole.[70] The relationship between poverty and health status is inextricably intertwined. Poverty increases the chance of poorer health status. Adverse living conditions, poor education, and poverty are associated with higher rates of alcoholism and other drug addiction.[71] Poor health, lack of access to primary care services, and multiple drug use often seen in women has a cumulative effect on the progression of addiction in women.[72]

A recent study conducted by Project HOPE's Center for Health Affairs[73] documented that the region has few options when it comes to treatment for alcohol and/or drug use. The study found that only 8 percent of distressed Appalachian counties had a provider of hospital-affiliated substance abuse outpatient services, and only 20 percent of distressed counties had hospital-affiliated mental health services. Nationwide, outpatient drug and/or alcohol treatment options have been decreasing in recent years, so it is not surprising that alcohol and/or drug use is particularly acute in Appalachia. Across the nation, the percentage of counties with hospital-affiliated outpatient drug and/or alcohol treatment fell from 29 percent in 1994 to 25 percent in 2000, according to the Project HOPE study.[74]

In the state where the study took place, 15 percent of families live below the federal poverty level, and in the specific county where the research took place there is a 32 percent poverty rate—the highest in the state. There are only two programs in the region that address the gender-specific and cultural needs of alcohol and/or drug using rural Appalachian women and their families.[75]

Typically small, remote, and with low populations, rural areas are often neglected in the creating of national political agendas or plans for reform and change. The problems of alcohol and/or drug use affect all segments of society, but weigh most heavily on the disadvantaged. These populations, consisting of both minorities and the poor, have the fewest resources to deal with problems of alcohol and/or drug use. They have the least access to services, both financial and physical; have the greatest incidence of impairment, disability, and death; and usually end up in the criminal justice and child welfare systems.[76] However, there are additional barriers found in Appalachia. These cultural barriers include a mistrust of outsiders, fear of the "system," the exclusion of specific groups in a bureaucracy, a tradition of self-sufficiency and taking care of one's own, as well as geographic and social isolation.[77]

Women in this geographic region are not adequately represented in the workforce; many stay at home to raise families or are underemployed. The more traditional the community, the more limited are the employment opportunities for women. The pink-collar jobs (service industries that include housekeepers, beauticians, waitresses, and child care providers) and the part-time positions that may be available rarely offer health care benefits. For women with children, the choice may be either to accept low wages without adequate health care or to remain unemployed and on public assistance with assured medical coverage for themselves and their children.[78]

Traditional barriers faced by many women who use alcohol and/or drugs in Appalachia were consistent among participants in this study: extreme poverty, lack of transportation, lack of child care, inability to pay for services, family violence, and low self-esteem.[79] Alcohol and/or drug use has been found to be one of the major long-term psychological effects of childhood sexual abuse.[80] In this study, eighteen of the twenty-five participants experienced sexual abuse in their childhoods, while three experienced violence with partners in adulthood. This finding mirrors other research[81] that suggests that many former addicts come from family backgrounds in which stories of abuse figure prominently. As this research shows, the daily struggle for survival is clearly visible in this area, and alcohol and/or drug use becomes a common way for participants to escape from the harsh realities of their lives.

Methods of Data Collection

The Sampling Design

The sampling design was purposive sampling. Purposive sampling looks for representativeness by choosing a sample that typifies the population, the theoretical category, or the phenomenon that is to be studied.[82] The sample in this study was chosen to enable me to investigate typical phenomena pertaining to theoretical issues of processes of rural Appalachian women's addiction and recovery, not to represent the population.[83]

Finding Participants

In preparation for my fieldwork, I contacted the addiction center in the area where I conducted the study and spoke to a counselor who kindly offered to distribute posters at the center and within the groups. I also contacted workers at the local women's shelter, who also put research posters in their agency. Posters calling for interested women to contact me were put up in grocery stores, beauty parlors, community malls, doctors' offices, churches, and a local gathering place in the community. Because this was a self-selective study, participants were free to call me and offer to be interviewed. Nine women responded to the advertisement I placed in the local paper. Another ten women were acquired through snowball sampling; that is, those I had interviewed recommended the study to others they knew. Snowball sampling is a useful technique because people are more likely to speak to a researcher if they know someone who has referred the researcher to them.[84] Five women responded to posters placed at various locations around the city. Finally, one participant heard about my study from an Alcoholics Anonymous (AA) member. Thirty-one women were screened, and the lack of at least eighteen months in recovery was the major reason for excluding six women from the study. Participants were given $25 (US) for their time.

Participants had to meet specific eligibility criteria before being selected for an interview. To ensure that participants were appropriate to my study, I used a form that asked screening questions when they telephoned me. When a woman called, I introduced myself over the phone and thanked her for her interest in participating in my study. Then I informed her about my study and about what types of questions I was interested in asking. I assured her that any information she told me over the phone would be kept confidential. I also informed her that she could ask me questions at any time during the phone call. Following this preamble, I asked the following screening questions: What was her present age?

At what age did she begin to use alcohol and/or drugs? What types of alcohol and/or drugs did she use? How long had she had problems with substances? And, finally, how long had she been in recovery?

To be part of this study, participants had to meet two criteria, namely that they had to be twenty years of age or older and that they had to have been in recovery for eighteen months or longer. The director at the local addiction center suggested that because eighteen is the age at which clients come to the center and because I wished to interview women who had been at least eighteen months in recovery, twenty years was the obvious starting age for participants at the time of our interviews. There are two advantages to interviewing women who had been abstinent for a period of at least eighteen months: (1) women are more likely to be stable in recovery after this period of time and, thus, more confident, and (2) because of this confidence, they are more likely to feel free to talk about past lives as women formerly addicted to alcohol and/or drugs. If those who called me met these inclusion criteria, I invited them to be interviewed.

The Interview Schedule and Process

After these women contacted me and expressed an interest in being interviewed, I set up a time, date, and place for us to meet. The setting of the interview was left to the discretion of participants, and all were comfortable meeting in my university office. A written consent form was available, which I explained to them before asking them to sign. I asked open-ended questions in this study while adhering to a semi-structured interview format, along with various probes to elicit information from participants on addiction and recovery processes.

As the interviews began, I first offered all participants the opportunity to choose pseudonyms, which all of them did. Second, I told them about my community work in Canada, assuring them that I had worked with women in similar situations and was aware of problems germane to women's experiences of addiction and recovery. The first part of the interview schedule involved completing a personal information sheet because I thought this might be useful information to use as a guideline to follow up on possible probes during our interviews. This schedule contained general demographic information that related specifically to age, marital status, children, employment, education, ethnic or cultural group, and religion. These queries were closed-ended and helped participants to describe their backgrounds.

The second part of the interview schedule, the questionnaire, consisted of their addiction narratives, which helped "set up" their general background in relation to alcohol and/or drug histories, providing the context in which to understand their experiences. This part of the schedule asked questions about past addiction, relating to the duration of use of alcohol and/or drugs, when participants first begin to use, why they used, their primary substance of choice, length of abstinence, and whether any members of their immediate family had ever used. I also asked them to clarify the meanings of the concepts "addiction" and "recovery." Following the addiction and recovery histories, they were asked to explain how they began addiction, how they managed to break addiction, how they began recovery and, finally, how they experienced or were experiencing abstinence.

Women's Involvement in the Interview Process

After transcribing the interviews, I returned them by mail to participants and incorporated their input into my final analysis. This was done in order to capture their perspectives accurately and to enable them to add further details or notes. I included a self-addressed stamped envelope and encouraged them to return transcripts to me if they wished, after adding any other information that was applicable. Only one participant availed herself of this opportunity.

Women's Backgrounds

Table 1.1 illustrates the women's demographic backgrounds. Their ages ranged between twenty and seventy-five years, with a median age of forty. Of the twenty-five women interviewed, twenty-two signified that their ethnic background was white and of English origin. One participant was of Cherokee descent, and two stated that they came from Italian and German backgrounds, respectively. Although all participants lived in the study area where the interviews took place, not all were born in the area.

Table 1.1. Participants' Personal Backgrounds

Variables	Frequency Percent	(n)
Age		
20–29	16.0	(4)
30–39	28.0	(7)
40–49	44.0	(11)
50+	12.0	(3)
Marital Status		
Single	32.0	(8)
Married	32.0	(8)
Divorced	28.0	(7)
Separated	8.0	(2)
Highest Education Attained		
High school	48.0	(12)
Community college	4.0	(1)
Some university	24.0	(6)
Completed university	20.0	(5)
Graduate degree	4.0	(1)

Continued on next page

Variables	Frequency Percent	(n)
Ethnic Group		
English	88.0	(22)
Other	12.0	(3)
Religious Affiliation		
Protestant	28.0	(7)
Catholic	20.0	(5)
Other	36.0	(9)
None	16.0	(4)
Occupation		
Professional	32.0	(8)
Service employee	24.0	(6)
No occupation (Student, homemaker, UI recipient, retired)	44.0	(11)
Net Income		
$0–9,999	44.0	(11)
$10,000–19,999	40.0	(10)
$20,000–29,999	4.0	(1)
$30,000–39,999	4.0	(1)
$40,000+	8.0	(2)

(n) = 25

At the time of the interviews, eight women were married, seven were divorced, eight were single, and two were going through difficult separations. Eight women had been married four times each, and five had been married twice before their present marriage. The number of children varied among participants. Eight women had no children, while seventeen of them had between one and six children each. Of these, three had five or six children each.

The highest education obtained by twelve participants was high school. One woman had graduated from a local community college. Six participants had some university education, while six had completed university, one woman with a graduate degree. Fourteen women were working when interviewed. These participants worked in such diverse areas as nursing, home care, counseling, teaching, housekeeping, day care, bartending, staffing specialization, and house painting. The remaining women (n=11) were not in the workforce at the time; that is, they were students at the local university, homemakers, retirees, or were on social welfare. Participants' employment was linked with income: the income of the eleven not employed fell below $10,000 (US) per year. Ten women had earned between $10,000 and $19,999 in the prior year, while the remainder (n=4) had incomes over $20,000, with one participant earning the largest salary, over $50,000, in her nursing career.

Religious affiliation varied among participants: seven were Protestant, five were of the Catholic faith, four signified that they had no religious affiliation, while the remainder (n=9) are members of the Episcopalian, Full Gospel Assembly, Christian Science, Pentecostal, or Baptist faith.

Summary

The research methodology directed this study to an investigation of rural Appalachian women's social processes of addiction and recovery. The focus of the analysis grew out of the issues and meanings that women attributed to their self changes in such processes. In the following chapter, I provide an overview of how women attribute meanings to themselves before they enter addiction and explore their experiences with alcohol and/or drugs. I also discuss how women initially construct alcohol and/or drug use in relation to themselves. Therefore, the following chapter highlights participants' narratives in the preexperimental and experimental phases and how this time, prior to entering addictive phases in earnest, is a problematic one for them.

Notes

1. J. Maxwell, *Qualitative Research Design: An Interactive Approach* (Thousand Oaks, CA: Sage, 1996), 58.
2. E. Comack, *Women in Trouble* (Halifax, Nova Scotia: Fernwood, 1996).
3. S. Kirby and K. McKenna, *Experience, Research, Social Change: Methods from the Margins* (Toronto, Ontario: Garamond, 1989).
4. C. Stivers, "Reflections on the Role of Personal Narrative in Social Science," *Signs: Journal of Women in Culture and Society* 18 (1993): 408–25.
5. H. Blumer, *Symbolic Interactionism: Perspective and Method* (Englewood Cliffs, NJ: Prentice Hall, 1969).
6. H. Schwartz and J. Jacobs, *Qualitative Sociology: A Method to the Madness* (New York: Macmillan, 1979), 25.
7. Blumer, *Symbolic Interactionism*, 325.
8. Schwartz and Jacobs, *Qualitative Sociology*, 25.
9. G. Lerner, *The Creation of Feminist Consciousness: From the Middle Ages to Eighteen-Seventy* (New York: Oxford University Press, 1993).
10. D. Smith, *The Everyday World as Problematic: A Feminist Sociology* (Toronto, Ontario: University of Toronto Press, 1987).
11. M. Sandmaier, *The Invisible Alcoholics: Women and Alcohol Use in America* (New York: McGraw-Hill, 1980).
12. K. Anderson and D. C. Jack, "Learning to Listen: Interview Techniques and Analyses," in *Women's Words: The Feminist Practice of Oral History*, ed. S. B. Gluck and D. Patai (New York: Routledge, 1991), 11–26.
13. K. Minister, "A Feminist Frame for the Oral History Interview," in *Women's Words: The Feminist Practice of Oral History*, ed. S. B. Gluck and D. Patai (New York: Routledge, 1991), 27–41.
14. S. Harding, *Feminism and Methodology* (Bloomington: Indiana University Press, 1987), 106.
15. C. Franz and A. Stewart, *Women Creating Lives: Identities, Resilience and Re-*

sistance (Boulder, CO: Westview, 1994).

16. P. H. Collins, *Black Feminist Thought: Knowledge, Consciousness, and the Politics of Empowerment* (New York: Routledge, 1990); C. Gilligan, *In a Different Voice: Psychological Theory and Women's Development* (Cambridge, MA: Harvard University Press, 1993).

17. Franz and Stewart, *Women Creating Lives;* Gilligan, *In a Different Voice.*

18. L. Code, *What Can She Know? Feminist Theory and the Construction of Knowledge* (Ithaca, NY: Cornell University Press, 1991); Franz and Stewart, *Women Creating Lives;* Gilligan, *In a Different Voice;* R. Josselson, *Revising Herself: The Story of Women's Identity from College to Midlife* (San Francisco, CA: Jossey-Bass, 1996); D. Smith, *Writing the Social: Critique, Theory and Investigations* (Toronto, Ontario: University of Toronto Press, 1999).

19. Smith, *Writing the Social.*

20. Code, *What Can She Know?* 190.

21. S. Reinharz, *Feminist Methods in Social Research* (New York: Oxford University Press, 1992), 173.

22. Reinharz, *Feminist Methods in Social Research,* 173.

23. B. Glaser and A. Strauss, *The Discovery of Grounded Theory: Strategies for Qualitative Research* (Chicago: Aldine, 1967).

24. *Semi-structured* refers to a research approach whereby the researcher plans to ask questions about a given topic but allows the data-gathering conversation itself to determine how the information is obtained. Feminist interview researchers often interchange the terms *unstructured, intensive, in-depth,* and *open-ended.* See Reinharz, *Feminist Methods in Social Research.*

25. H. Graham, "Surveying through Stories," in *Social Researching: Politics, Problems, Practice,* ed. C. Bell and H. Roberts (London: Routledge, 1984), 112.

26. Anderson and Jack, "Learning to Listen," 17.

27. T. Horne, *Making a Difference: Program Evaluation for Health Promotion* (Edmonton, Alberta: WellQuest Consulting, 1995).

28. L. A. Hoff, *Battered Women as Survivors* (London: Routledge, 1990).

29. M. McMahon, *Engendering Motherhood: Identity and Self-Transformation in Women's Lives* (New York: Guilford, 1995).

30. J. Charon, *Symbolic Interactionism: An Introduction, an Interpretation, an Integration,* seventh ed. (Upper Saddle River, NJ: Prentice Hall, 2001).

31. Glaser and Strauss, *Discovery of Grounded Theory.*

32. Stivers, "Reflections," 408.

33. Stivers, "Reflections," 412.

34. Stivers, "Reflections," 412.

35. Stivers, "Reflections," 420.

36. Leslie Levine, *Codependent Forevermore* (Chicago: University of Chicago Press, 1999).

37. L. Levesque-Lopman, *Claiming Reality: Phenomenology and Women's Experience* (Totowa, NJ: Rowman and Littlefield, 1988).

38. A. Stewart, "Toward a Feminist Strategy for Studying Women's Lives," in *Women Creating Lives: Identities, Resilience, and Resistance,* ed. C. Franz and A. Stewart (Boulder, CO: Westview, 1994), 11–35.

39. Franz and Stewart, *Women Creating Lives.*

40. Stewart, "Toward a Feminist Strategy," 11–35.

41. E. Ettorre, *Women and Substance Use* (London: Macmillan, 1992); E. Goode, *Drugs in American Society,* fifth ed. (Boston: McGraw-Hill, 1999); M. Rosenbaum, *Women and Drugs: Twenty-five Years of Research and Policy* (San Francisco: Lindesmith Center, 1998).

42. J. Grant, *The Women and Substance Abuse Report (WASA): The Invisible Problem* (Moncton, New Brunswick: Support to Single Parents, 1997).

43. Stewart, "Toward a Feminist Strategy," 11.

44. Personal Narratives Group, ed., *Interpreting Women's Lives: Feminist Theory and Personal Narratives* (Bloomington: Indiana University Press, 1989).

45. Stewart, "Toward a Feminist Strategy," 11.

46. Stewart, "Toward a Feminist Strategy," 30.

47. N. Van Den Bergh, "Having Bitten the Apple: A Feminist Perspective on Addictions," in *Feminist Perspectives on Addiction*, ed. N. Van Den Bergh (New York: Springer, 1991), 5.

48. Van Den Bergh, "Having Bitten the Apple," 5.

49. J. Maxwell, *Qualitative Research Design: An Interactive Approach* (Thousand Oaks, CA: Sage, 1996), 58; Reinharz, *Feminist Methods in Social Research*, 173.

50. Maxwell, *Qualitative Research Design*, 58.

51. D. Crooks, "The Importance of Symbolic Interaction in Grounded Theory Research on Women's Health," *Health Care for Women International* 22 (2001): 11–28; Ettorre, *Women and Substance Use*.

52. Crooks, "Importance of Symbolic Interaction," 4.

53. Crooks, "Importance of Symbolic Interaction," 9.

54. A. A. Abbot, "Substance Use and the Feminist Perspective," in *Feminist Practice in the 21st Century*, ed. N. Van Den Bergh (Washington, DC: National Association of Social Workers Press, 1995): 258–78; N. Campbell, *Gender, Drug Policy, and Social Justice: Using Women* (New York: Routledge, 2000); Van Den Bergh, "Having Bitten the Apple," 3–30.

55. C. Grella and V. Joshi, "Gender Differences in Drug Treatment Careers among Clients in the National Drug Use Treatment Outcome Study," *American Journal of Drug and Alcohol Use* 25 (1999): 385.

56. C. A. Dell and K. Garabedian, *Canadian Community Epidemiology Network on Drug Use: 2002 National Report* (Ottawa, Ontario: Canadian Center on Substance Use, 2003).

57. Campbell, *Gender, Drug Policy, and Social Justice;* M. Plant, *Women and Alcohol: Contemporary and Historical Perspectives* (London: Free Association Books, 1997).

58. J. Blackwell, W. E. Thurston, and K. Graham, "Women's Use of Alcohol, Tobacco and Other Drugs in Canada," in *Canadian Women and Substance Use: Overview and Policy Implications*, ed. M. Adrian, C. Lundy, and M. Eliany (Toronto, Ontario: Addiction Research Foundation, 1996), 229.

59. J. Clark, "The Historical Context of Medicalization and Gender: Its Relationship to Alcohol and Other Drug Use in Canada," in *Women's Use of Alcohol, Tobacco and Other Drugs in Canada*, ed. M. Adrian, C. Lundy, and M. Eliany (Toronto, Ontario: Addiction Research Foundation, 1996), 14–20.

60. H. Becker, *Outsiders* (New York: Free Press, 1963); P. Biernacki, *Pathways from Heroin Addiction: Recovery without Treatment* (Philadelphia: Temple University Press, 1986); N. Denzin, *The Recovering Alcoholic* (Newbury Park, CA: Sage, 1987b); J. Haas, *Seeking Bliss: The Study of Addiction and Recovery* (Victoria, British Columbia: Mosaic, 2003).

61. M. Rosenbaum, *Women on Heroin* (New Brunswick, NJ: Rutgers University Press, 1981).

62. S. Murphy and M. Rosenbaum, *Pregnant Women on Drugs: Combating Stereotypes and Stigma* (New Brunswick, NJ: Rutgers University Press, 1999).

63. P. Raine, *Women's Perspectives on Drugs and Alcohol: The Vicious Circle*, (Hampshire, England: Ashgate, 2001).

64. See Abbot, "Substance Use and the Feminist Perspective," 258–78; L. Beckman,

"Self-Esteem of Women Alcoholics," *Journal of Studies on Alcohol* 39 (1978): 491–98; W. T. Bernard, *Including Black Women in Health and Social Policy Development: Winning over Addictions; Empowering Black Mothers with Addictions to Overcome Triple Jeopardy* (Halifax, Nova Scotia: Maritime Centre of Excellence for Women's Health, 2001); L. Blood and A. Cornwall, "Childhood Sexual Victimization as a Factor in the Treatment of Substance Misusing Adolescents," *Substance Use and Misuse* 31 (1996): 1015–39; S. Blume, "Alcohol and Drug Problems in Women: Old Attitudes, New Knowledge," in *Treatment Choices for Alcoholism and Substance Abuse*, ed. H. Milkman and L. Sederer (Toronto, Ontario: Lexington Books, 1990), 183–98; D. D. Celentano and D. McQueen, "Multiple Substance Use among Women with Alcohol-Related Problems," in *Alcohol Problems in Women,* ed. S. C. Wilsnack and L. J. Beckman (New York: Guilford, 1984); Ettorre, *Women and Substance Use;* K. Graham, V. Carver, and P. J. Brett, "Alcohol and Drug Use by Older Women: Results of a National Survey," *Canadian Journal of Aging* 14 (1995): 769–91; S. M. Grover and S. P. Thomas, "Substance Use and Anger in Mid-life Women," *Issues in Mental Health Nursing* 14 (1993): 19–29; S. M. Lammers, D. E. H. Mainzer, and H. M. M. Breteler, "Submission and Rebellion: Excessive Drinking of Women in Problematic Heterosexual Partner Relationships," *International Journal of the Addictions* 30 (1995): 901–17; A. Long and B. Mullen, "An Exploration of Women's Perceptions of the Major Factors That Contributed to Their Alcohol Abuse," *Journal of Advanced Nursing* 19 (1994): 623–39; B. A. Miller and W. R Downs, "The Impact of Family Violence on the Use of Alcohol by Women," *Alcohol Health and Research World* 17 (1993): 137–43.

65. Levine, *Codependent Forevermore.*

66. S. Brown, *Treating the Alcoholic: A Developmental Model of Recovery* (New York: John Wiley and Sons, 1985); Rosenbaum, *Women on Heroin;* R. Stevens, *The Street Addict Role: A Theory of Heroin Addiction* (Albany: State University of New York Press, 1991); C. Terry, *The Fellas: Overcoming Prison and Addiction* (Belmont, CA: Wadsworth/Thomson Learning, 2003).

67. National Rural Health Association, *Policy Brief* (Kansas City, MO: National Rural Health Association, 2005.

68. M. A. Rosswurm, "Illness Experiences and Health Recovery Behaviors of Patients in Southern Appalachia," *Western Journal of Nursing Research* 18 (1996): 44–61.

69. T. Tatum, "Rural Women's Recovery Program and Women's Outreach" *Substance Abuse and Mental Health Services Administration, Center for Substance Abuse Treatment,* http://www.treatment.org/TAPS/TAP17/tap17rural.html (May 16, 2006).

70. B. Portnoy, "Healthy People in Rural America by the Year 2000," in *Sowing Seeds in the Mountains: Community-Based Coalitions for Cancer Prevention and Control*, ed. R. A. Couto, N. K. Simpson, and G. Harris (Bethesda, MD: National Institutes of Health, National Cancer Institute, 1995), 102–19.

71. Department of Health and Human Services, *Alcohol and Health: Seventh Report to Congress* (Rockville, MD: Department of Health and Human Services, 1990).

72. Tatum, "Rural Women's Recovery Program and Women's Outreach."

73. J. C. Stensland, C. Mueller, and J. Sutton, "An Analysis of the Financial Conditions of Health Care Institutions in the Appalachian Region and Their Economic Impacts" (Bethesda, MD: Project HOPE Center for Health Affairs, 2002).

74. Stensland, Mueller, and Sutton, "Analysis of the Financial Conditions of Health Care Institutions."

75. Stensland, Mueller, and Sutton, "Analysis of the Financial Conditions of Health Care Institutions."

76. Tatum, "Rural Women's Recovery Program and Women's Outreach."

77. Tatum, "Rural Women's Recovery Program and Women's Outreach."

78. Tatum, "Rural Women's Recovery Program and Women's Outreach."

79. Tatum, "Rural Women's Recovery Program and Women's Outreach."

80. Blood and Cornwall, "Childhood Sexual Victimization"; J. Copeland, "A Qualitative Study of Self-Managed Change in Substance Dependence among Women," *Contemporary Drug Problems* 25 (Summer 1998): 321–43; Grella and Joshi, "Gender Differences in Drug Treatment Careers," 385; Long and Mullen, "Exploration of Women's Perceptions," 623–39.

81. Denzin, *Alcoholic Self;* Haas, *Seeking Bliss;* Rosenbaum, *Women on Heroin.*

82. McMahon, *Engendering Motherhood.*

83. McMahon, *Engendering Motherhood.*

84. P. Li, *Social Research Methods: An Introduction* (Toronto, Ontario: Butterworth, 1981).

Chapter 2

The Preaddicted Self

Introduction

> The use of substances is never independent of the complex web of meaning within which they are embedded.[1]

This chapter considers rural Appalachian women's accounts of their lives before they become addicted to alcohol and/or drugs. This study afforded the opportunity to explore the major factors that impact on participants' lives in their preexperimental and experimental phases. It is also possible to explore the ways in which participants explain how individual and social selves come about, that is, how they make meanings of themselves in these various phases through influential factors that they consider important in their lives. In this section, I present a close analysis of how women's views of themselves emerge, along with the multiple problems they experience before they begin addictive careers in earnest.

Individuals within society actively construct social worlds by making meaning, and human behavior is an active process of interpretation and negotiation in which meanings are created and attached to objects, situations, and events in social environments.[2] Meaning-making is neither universally held nor permanently fixed. Meanings are properties that individuals convey upon the social world in the processes of social interaction. The ways in which people define social situations and give meaning to them are sociologically important.[3]

Therefore, because the use of alcohol and/or drugs is dependent on *how* individuals make use of such substances, they represent different things to different people. For example, drugs are used as medication to numb pain during surgery or to promote pleasure for emotional release. And they are often used in religious ceremonies in various cultures. For example, members of certain Native American churches ingest peyote cactus (a psychoactive substance) during ceremonies,[4] and the coca leaf is chewed for pleasure and relaxation within Inca culture.[5]

The meanings participants attach to their use of alcohol and/or drugs and the personal changes they experience do not arise independently of the contexts in which they were embedded. The use of substances is tied to local interactional settings as well as to larger social structural dimensions of social life.[6] In this study, *structure* implies a system of patterned social relations within which participants interact with selves and others. An individual's structural social position influences her consciousness, experiences, social networks, opportunities, and dispositions. Individuals may operate freely in structured environments, but not necessarily under freely chosen circumstances.[7]

Thus, participants' behaviors shape and are shaped by experiences within the contexts of structured social relations. By listening to women's voices and narratives, I try to understand and articulate the meanings they give as they talk about their initial and ongoing experiences before their alcohol and/or drug use becomes problematic. Alcohol and/or drug use are many things to many people, and understanding women's meanings toward themselves in their preexperimental and experimental phase is critical to understanding their dependency phases and, ultimately, their recovery processes and ongoing abstinence.

Alcohol and/or drug use may arise out of peer and familial relations and may be mediated by social class and cultural norms. Social structure provides the rules and resources involved in human action, both enabling individuals to act and constraining them from acting in certain ways.[8] Social actions and interactions are constrained by, yet generative of, the structural dimensions of social reality.[9] The structural location of a person in society, including family environments, mediates that person's use of substances. From this perspective, I argue that the structural location of participants is critically important to understanding their experiences with alcohol and/or drugs as well as their recovery processes. Therefore, I focus attention on the importance of participants' social context and meanings as influencing their use of such substances. From this perspective, use of alcohol and/or drugs is seen not as singularly aberrant, but as a means by which they create meanings[10] and establish individual and social identities in preaddiction, addiction, and recovery processes.

To better understand the social processes through which rural women in this study shift from the role of addict to that of nonaddict, I divide their experiences into three analytically distinct phases: (1) *The Preaddicted Self*, (2) *The Addicted Self*, and (3) *The Recovering Self*. *The Preaddicted Self* as discussed in this chapter pertains to the preexperimental phase in which social processes in women's lives lead them to experiment with alcohol and/or drugs for various reasons and on various levels. *The Addicted Self* as outlined in chapter 3 refers to the processes whereby these women become immersed in alcohol and/or drug culture and develop concepts of themselves as addicts, while in chapter 4, *The Recovering Self* refers to the processes by which women begin to consider recovery and struggle to stay abstinent.

The Preexperimental Self

> People build up and construct their behavior based on the meaning they attribute to the particular situations in which they find themselves.[11]

A woman who uses alcohol and/or drugs faces the necessity of rebuilding herself and her life around her use of such substances. It is in this respect that the process of becoming addicted provides the context in this chapter for understanding how women initially construct the meanings they attribute to their selves and to their alcohol and/or drug use. I argue that one cannot understand women's recovery unless one first understands how women view preaddicted selves as they begin to experiment with alcohol and/or drug use and, eventually, move into addictive phases.

Participants' descriptions of themselves in *The Preexperimental Self* phase show that they often evaluate themselves in terms of how they are seen by significant others and that they internalize these evaluations into individual self-images. Their descriptions highlight how the two aspects of themselves, their individual and social identities, are interrelated and mutually interacting. In the following section, I explore descriptors that highlight participants' feelings and emotions during the time before experimentation begins.

As Sandstrom et al.[12] argue, people behave in situations according to the meanings they give to those situations. The meanings given to particular situations emerge out of ongoing interactions. Such fluidity is mediated in social contexts and is anchored in behaviors. In its understanding of human action, symbolic interactionism focuses on interactions, including social interactions and interactions with one's self. This perspective emphasizes the idea that people define their environments rather than simply respond to them; humans are forever dynamic and active rather than static and passive. Individuals are "emergent,"[13] always changing as they deal with situations. What people do in particular situations depends on their definitions of such situations. The central importance of perspective determines how a person acts in given situations. Perspectives define the world: they are social, dynamic, and guiding.[14] In this view, a person does not simply respond to their environment, but defines it, acts toward it, and uses it according to the way in which that person defines the situations.

This theoretical perspective of how individuals define and make meanings within various social contexts allowed me to explore processes through which participants gave meanings to the alcohol and/or drugs they used and to examine how these meanings and their situated contexts shaped their use of such substances. This perspective facilitated my exploration of the processes of self changes and the antecedents of these changes for participants.

The goal of this section is to understand the basic social and social-psychological processes that characterized participants' preexperimental self phases. Consideration of participants' upbringings and their experiences before their alcohol and/or drug experimentations provided relevant insights into how they viewed themselves in their family environments.

One of the salient questions in the interviews was what kind of lives participants had lived before they began to experiment with alcohol and/or drugs. By listening to how these women perceived themselves in *The Preexperimental Self* phase, I came to a greater understanding of how they began their processes of using in the early phases of addiction.

Overall, I was interested in the answers to two questions regarding participants' preexperimental lives: (1) who were these women before they became involved in alcohol and/or drug culture, and (2) what were their lives like within their social environments during this time? The following discussion highlights participants' preexperimental phases within family backgrounds.

Women's Family Backgrounds

As participants talked about their early years, it became clear that their family backgrounds were diverse. For example, twelve women had grown up in families in which their parents did not divorce when the participants were young. These participants talked about both parents being employed or about their mothers working within the home. Ten of the participants had grown up in single-parent households in which their primary caregivers had been their mothers throughout their youth, and three had grown up with stepfathers who were married to their mothers. The single-parent mothers were single through divorce or death, or because they initially had not been married. Participants who had grown up with single-parent mothers mentioned the difficulties their mothers experienced in trying to raise the children alone. Only two made note of the fact that they grew up in poor families.

Two participants had been adopted immediately after birth, and three had lost their fathers when they were very young. Six participants had grown up with more than seven other siblings in the home.

Although participants' backgrounds differed in many ways, the following five common characteristics emerged from women's narratives: (1) Thirteen participants had experienced either sexual or physical abuse by family members in *The Preexperimental Self* phase. Fathers, grandfathers, stepfathers, and brothers had perpetrated the abuse. Only one participant noted that her mother had been abusive to her in her younger years. For two of the older participants who had become addicted in later years, it was husbands or partners who had been abusive toward them. (2) Thirteen participants stated that they also had witnessed violence perpetrated against their mothers by fathers and/or mothers' partners. (3) Six stated that they had felt abandoned, disconnected, or isolated due to various factors in their family environments (i.e., adoption, death of a parent, or rejection). (4) Six stated that they came from, as one woman said, "a good family." Their entry into *The Preexperimental Self* phase was due to peer and/or sibling influences. (5) Twenty-one participants had family members who used alcohol and/or drugs to varying degrees. Although some families used sporadically, such use was common in participants' family environments. This seems to indicate that alcohol and/or drug use was a learned behavior that was passed on to participants at an early age. Family members were fathers, grandfathers, uncles, brothers, and stepfathers. In four of these participants' families, mothers also used alcohol and/or drugs. The following table shows the number of addicted family members for participants.

Four participants had no family members who used alcohol and/or drugs in any way. A plurality of participants (n=12) had one or two family members who used, and 9 had three or more. Family members' addictions included alcohol and marijuana, but not hard drugs, such as cocaine or heroin. This mirrors participants' own use of alcohol and/or drugs: twenty of them stressed that alcohol and/or marijuana were the drugs of choice from which they subsequently recovered.

Table 2.1. Addicted Family Members

Number of addicted family members	Frequency percent	(n)
0	16.0	(4)
1	24.0	(6)
2	24.0	(6)
3	8.0	(2)
4	0.0	(0)
5+	28.0	(7)
Total:	100.0	(25)

I begin this section by discussing various descriptors by which participants characterized early feelings about themselves. I deal here specifically with participants' perceptions as they look back at their experiences in *The Preexperimental Self* phase and with the relevance of these perceptions to participants' initial alcohol and/or drug use. Because my study is based on social-psychological assumptions of participants' activities, my data indicate social worlds prior to alcohol and/or drug use: the social worlds to which women belonged. This includes relationships to families of origin, which, ultimately, affected their relationships to themselves. The concept of social world as defined by Lindesmith, Strauss, and Denzin is useful:

> Social worlds [are] groupings of individuals bound together by networks of community or universes of discourse. . . . Members share symbolizations . . . and also share perspectives on "reality." The concept is applicable to almost any collectivity—including families—if we emphasize communication and membership, for membership is not merely a matter of physical or official belonging, but of shared symbolization, experiences, and interests.[15]

This aspect of participants' lives involved socialization processes within alcohol and/or drug culture. These socialization processes had a direct bearing on their addiction. A sense of membership in a social world that consisted of other users was important to participants at this phase. Individuals all experience different types of social worlds: in the early years, it is the family's world that exercises influence; in the school world, peers become significant; and, in the adult world, occupations/jobs and coworkers are often salient. Social worlds provide the bases for social circumstances.

Participants talked about many factors that influenced their behaviors, perceptions, and feelings in *The Preexperimental Self* phase. The women used a wide range of insightful adjectives and phrases to characterize how they felt about themselves. From these descriptions, one can see that participants viewed themselves in a negative fashion: feelings of self-hate, depression, low self-esteem, and unworthiness were common. Not one woman evaluated herself positively in this phase. Participants' descriptions of themselves related to self-esteem, self-concept, and evaluations of how circumstances in families of origin were affecting them at the time. The first quotes discussed below are taken from women whose family context included family violence. They are followed by quotes from those who came from families in which there were no experiences of sexual or physical violence.

Women Who Experienced Violence within the Home

The following table illustrates the number and percentage of participants who experienced violence within their homes.

Table 2.2. Violence within the Home

Family member	Frequency percent	(n)
Male	52.0	(13)
Mother	4.0	(1)
Husband/partner	8.0	(2)
Total:	64.0	(16)

As table 2.2 highlights, thirteen participants experienced sexual and/or physical violence from male family members, including fathers, grandfathers, stepfathers, and brothers, while one participant experienced physical abuse from her mother. Two participants who were older when they became addicted experienced violence from their husbands or partners.

Most literature on woman abuse focuses almost exclusively on urban areas, and rural woman abuse has been somewhat neglected in the literature on violence against women.[16] However, several studies[17] have recognized and documented this problem. There are many disadvantages to girls and women within rural environments that pertain to violence: rural communities define the roles of women and men more narrowly than urban communities,[18] rural women receive lower pay than women in urban areas,[19] and the division of labor is more stereotypically gendered[20] in that rural women are more rigidly tied to housework and child care.[21] So, too, are the images of rural women more intimately tied up with religious culture. Geographical isolation in rural communities magnifies the subordination and loneliness of women in the home; and rural women are cut off from beneficial services of the state, such as health care and social services, public transportation, independent housing, educational opportunities, and licensed child care.[22] A recent qualitative exploratory study on sexual assault committed by former husbands or cohabitants in the lives of rural women in Ohio found that these women suffered multiple serious sexual assaults and experienced other harms, including psychological assaults and the destruction of prized objects.[23] It is not surprising, then, that many participants in my study experienced violence in their younger years and some as women in their adult lives.

Nancy experienced violence in her family of origin. She talked about how her early perception of herself came from the notion that the abuse she was experiencing indicated a particular place for her within her family. She saw herself as some "thing," a "vessel," to be used, thus leading to profound negative individual and social feelings toward herself. This resulted in her feeling that she was an object of use within her family:

> Well, I was molested, I was ah, emotionally used, I was raped. I was molested by my grandpa. I was emotionally used by my father, by my whole family pretty much. I was raped by my first boyfriend, I mean this, um, the molestation just kind of set up this cycle of all this shit happening, and I thought it was my fault. I finally figured out it wasn't my fault. I didn't deserve to be treated that way. I thought that all I was, was just some vessel to be used. That was so painful to go through.

Nancy highlighted how she always felt "shame" from her parents, as well: they had to marry because her mother was pregnant with her at the time. She internalized this shame and stated that she always "hated" herself because of these circumstances. She stressed in the interview that she perceived that her parents blamed her for their indiscretion:

> I was ashamed. See, my Mom and Dad had to marry because of me and that was a shame and whenever they looked at me, they saw what they perceived as their shame and they took it out on me and they weren't, they weren't even aware of it. I mean I'm not angry with them about it anymore cause they're, they're so unaware of what they did, they just kind of walk around blindly but that's what they did, and I can't change that. And I had such self-hate because of that.

Sandy is another participant whose lifestyle was similar. She talked about how she was brought up in a family in which all the members were, and still are, alcohol and drug addicts (using marijuana and alcohol) and dealers. She experienced this type of environment as a child, and sexual abuse when she was older. She commented on her family background:

> You see, with my family, um, they're mostly all drug dealers so like if I could, if I went to my sister's right now, it's guaranteed there is

> two or three joints going around the table all the time, non-stop. I was given alcohol as a child. My parents were big drinkers. Lots of times my step-dad got mad at my Mom because she would leave. He would have us sit there and get drunk with him. So, really five is when that was going on.

Sandy related how she believed as a child that "[t]here wasn't nothing wrong with smoking marijuana, there wasn't nothing wrong with marijuana. I thought it was normal to sit around the kitchen table and smoke a joint. I mean kids or no kids; I just thought it was normal." When I asked Sandy how she felt before she began to experiment with drugs, she said: "Oh, I used to beat myself to death all the time, call myself names and I used to feel that I was totally worthless. I used to be really suicidal." When I asked why she felt this way, she stated: "Why? I didn't have very good parents. They were, I had three different stepfathers. I was sexually abused from [age] one to seventeen. There was lots and lots of violence in the home."

Violence was a constant in Tracy's life. She left home by the time she was twelve and was institutionalized until she was sixteen for, among other things, violence and truancy. When I asked her to relate to me her early family life, it was easy to see how angry she still was about her early circumstances: in fact, her anger was palpable. This was a result of the incestuous abuse she experienced in her early years. She almost spat out her words about herself and about her childhood experiences as I asked her:

> Q: What was your upbringing like? Did you have a good childhood?
> Tracy: No, no. I'm a product of forcive sexual abuse, incest, and physical abuse.
> Q: From whom?
> Tracy: My stepfather, ah, he did, incest, and my stepfather beat me.
> Q: At what ages did that occur?
> Tracy: Always—I don't ever *not* remember it [participant's emphasis].

Another participant, Theresa, stated that her perception of herself came about through her "horrible" environment, in which she lacked any connection with her mother:

> I had a horrible environment at the time [before using]. My mother was with this guy and I mean he was, he was in control of everything. He was in control of my mother. Basically, I did not have my mother for a period of probably four years. Yeah, yeah. I didn't like myself then. I didn't like myself at all. I hate my past.

Hannah also had a family environment that consisted of violence. Her father was abusive toward her mother, and the atmosphere in the household was unpleasant and stressful for all concerned. As Hannah narrated her story, it was easy to see how she internalized the abuse she witnessed toward her mother toward herself:

> I had low self-esteem. Probably because of the way my dad treated my mother, the way he talked to her. It was a short marriage. I was six years old when they divorced, but the only thing I remember of that marriage is my father coming in every day from work and my mom would be working in the kitchen, cooking dinner and everything, and I have this picture of him standing in the doorway, coming in and just railing. Just totally railing her and everything. Screaming at her and he was physically abusive, verbally abusive. I remember sitting out in the hallway, just sort of in that autistic mode, and I remember like my stomach hurt, God, my stomach hurt, being just so sick.

Hannah also lost her "best friend" while she was in high school. This event eventually compelled her to shut off, or to internalize, her feelings: "I had clenched off all my emotions. I was like the walking dead. It was like, you know, just, um, felt nothing. I felt nothing. If there was something hurting in me, like any physical or emotional pain, I would just stuff it down further. I would just stuff it in." It is probably no wonder, then, that Hannah continued by stating: "I have always dealt with low self-esteem, searching, trying to find an identity."

One of the older participants, Martha, stressed her feelings of unworthiness as she talked about how her abusive husband, after many years of a compatible marriage until the abuse began, made her feel like "one miserable wife, [as] I could never do anything right." As I asked her about this, she responded:

> Q: This unworthiness, this came from your marriage and the husband that was abusing you?
> Martha: I think so. Oh, I'm sure because I could never do anything right. I couldn't even bake pies to please him.

Marie was another participant who experienced violence in her family, but it was her mother who was abusive to her and her sister. When Marie was fourteen, she also experienced sexual abuse by a family member and then rape, followed by marriage to an abusive husband. She said:

> After my sister was born and within a couple of years, my mum developed schizophrenia. And in the 70s they didn't have very good treatment for it, so the side affects from the medicine she was on made her abusive—verbally, physically, mentally. I always felt like I had to protect my little sister. I was always scared, so there was a lot of abuse growing up. And I knew that was the beginning. Right when I was probably fourteen or something, I was sexually molested by a member of the family—an older male and my sister was too and that was pretty traumatic and then at seventeen, I was raped, and at eighteen, I got married to an abusive husband.

Marie continued: "I never did feel loved except for my Grandma and she died and really, I still felt unloved." It can be argued that in Marie's early life, as well as in those of other participants, the treatment they received in their families laid the groundwork for negative feelings of self-worth.

Another woman, Robbie, also experienced long-term sexual abuse, beginning at age six, from her older brother and his friends: "It was long-term, for me long-term, lots of perpetrators. My youngest brother who was six years older than I, he was my long-term perpetrator. By the time I was six, he was bringing his friends home to abuse me." When I asked Robbie why she did not tell her parents about this she stated that her brother had threatened to kill their parents if she did. As she stated: "When you are six years old, you believe everything your older brother tells you." Therefore, she was too afraid to inform her parents about her brother's abuse. Along with this abuse, her parents also managed to "trade" her for a mobile home, treating her as an object to be used.

> My mother wanted a one-bedroom mobile home. They were looking at retirement because my mother was thirty-six when I was born. My dad was forty-four and they were looking for a retirement place, and my mother decided I was an extra and she had found this one-bedroom mobile home that she liked and she wanted that.

Robbie continued by stressing that her life certainly was not her own at this time: she had no control over her life and she could not finish high school. It is obvious that Robbie had not been able to assert any identity of her own in her family environment:

> My parents had kind of given me away when I was fifteen to this man and all I ever wanted to do was finish high school. I just wanted to finish high school and none of that worked out. It was all so out of control, such a feeling of being out of control, that my life wasn't mine.

Another participant, Grace, also highlighted the abuse she received from her husband, as well as abuse directed toward her children. These were experiences she was having difficulty handling: "My, ah, husband, my children's father, ah, whenever he abused me and everything and he abused my children. I couldn't handle it and deal with it."

Susan talked about how her cousin sexually abused her when she was twelve. She continued in her narrative to expand on how she attached no blame to her cousin for this experience:

> Susan: My own cousin got me pregnant.
> Q: How did that happen?
> Susan: Well, I wouldn't call it abuse. I mean we were almost the same age. He was thirteen, I was twelve. He's my cousin. I mean it's not like he beat me or anything. I just kind of woke up to have him being on top of me. So I wouldn't really call it abuse. I'd say it's more or less like, watching my language carefully, a dumb, fuck moment.

All participants who experienced some type of family violence (n=13) felt the repercussions of their experiences, which, as stated above, included negative evaluations of themselves. Familial experiences affected women's self-identities and definitions of who they really were. There was little healthy familial support and no positive role modeling during this time for those participants who experienced such violence. Such support is a key ingredient in every individual's physical and psychological health.[24] Socialization is the lifelong process through which individuals acquire self-identities and learn the physical, mental, and social skills necessary for survival in society. The kind of person one becomes depends greatly on what one learns during the formative years from surrounding social groups and social environments. During infancy and early childhood, family support and guidance are central to a child's developing self-concept. In some families, children grow up in an environment of mutual trust, emotional warmth, and a sense of security.[25]

In other families, however, children grow up in settings characterized by fear, danger, and risks created by parental neglect, emotional maltreatment, or sexual demands. Abused children often experience low self-esteem, the inability to trust others, feelings of isolation, powerlessness, and denial of their feelings.[26] No matter what form the abuse takes, it represents a complete breakdown of the trust and interdependence that ought to exist in any healthy relationship. Such assaults can be seen as assaults on these participants' "core personhoods,"[27] or a scarring of their selves. Not surprisingly, participants stated that low self-esteem and depression were common factors in their lives prior to addiction. Participants had suicidal thoughts, and eight actually attempted suicide as young girls.

Women Who Did Not Experience Violence in Their Homes

For the six participants who did not experience violent familial backgrounds, self-evaluations were also negative, due to varying factors. A case in point is Kathleen, whose quote indicates how her negative view of herself came about in her preexperimental self phase:

> There were a lot of things happening in my family at that time [before her drug use]. My Dad's an alcoholic; I had easy access to it. My Dad had a heart attack. Looking back I think that affected me a lot. There was a lot of craziness around the house at the time. So I got to the point where I was suicidal again. I was thinking in terms of, um, I couldn't stand being inside of me anymore. So I had a suicide attempt.

Kathleen continued by stating that, as a young girl, she tried to commit suicide three times because she was "very unhappy" and was having trouble making "sense of her world." Obviously this was a very discomforting and stressful time for her.

Two participants, Susan and Mary, questioned their sense of who they were in their early lives after being adopted as babies. Through this experience, the two women saw themselves as a "problem." For example, Susan, who had experienced sexual abuse from her cousin when she was twelve years old, talked about being born with a disorder that had profound consequences for her. Doctors had not thought she would survive to be two years old. As Susan talked to me, it was only at the end of the interview that she told me about her early life in the hospital. It was obvious that she was still angry at her birth parents, who gave her up for adoption:

> Sometimes I get really depressed. Knowing that my real parents had no frigging idea at all how to take care of a kid. If they had had some kind of clue, they wouldn't have given me up. They looked at me as a problem and that just blows my brain. Sometimes, I get really depressed.

Mary's story is especially poignant, as I see her as a young woman who is still trying to make sense of why her mother gave her up for adoption. She talked about this aspect of her early life throughout the entire interview, referring back to it many times as she told me her story. Her mother had become pregnant with twins, Mary and her brother, as a result of a relationship with a married man. Shortly after birth, both Mary and her brother were "signed off" by their mother, who had gone to a home for unwed mothers. Relatives told Mary that her mother had had to give her up because if she did not, her mother would not get her inheritance, and her family would have disowned her. So, as Mary said:

> Before the addiction, my brain was like fragmented, or there was something distorted in the perception of myself. I don't think I ever personally felt like myself, I mean, I knew I was adopted since the time I was five and that affected me greatly and, you know, sometimes, I'm real good at beating myself up.

A feeling of difference is highlighted in Lynn's story. Although her family was seemingly normal, and there was no family violence, Lynn felt "different" in her family because of the way her parents treated her in relation to her sister:

> My sister was perfect. Straight "A" student, graduated magna cum laude from honors college, had full scholarships, got a master's degree in three years. She's a genius, okay. There's no competing with that. So I was always in trouble, I was always bad, I didn't do anything right. [Her parents would say,] "Why can't you be more like your sister?"

She said that she felt she did not "fit in" with her family because of her dyslexia, which her family did not seem to know about:

> I never felt normal, and they were all intelligent, educated reading types and here I was, I was very cute as a child, but to them, cute was not important. It's being educated and being able to read. I was dys-

> lexic, which I never told my parents. It took me years to try to figure out why I couldn't read in school and I'd have to read letters one at a time. I never told anyone this, you know. I was just very careful about how I did everything cause I knew I wasn't doing it the way other kids were.

Another participant, Esther, validated her feelings about her early adulthood as she clarified how she felt about herself in her preexperimental self phase. Such feelings resulted in her becoming bulimic and anorexic:

> I had very low self-esteem for my whole life. I have no idea where it came from. Very, very low self-esteem. Ah, I was always thinking, what are people thinking of me? How am I being viewed? Um, always had weight issues. I was bulimic for a period, anorexic for a period. And then what they call, bulimic-anorexic. I didn't like my body then, I never had a lot of self-confidence even in elementary school.

Rivka narrated a story of feelings of isolation due not only to being "bullied" by her sister and her sister's friends at a young age but also to a lack of friends as she was growing up. Rivka felt a sense of unworthiness in her early life, which she internalized from a significant other in her life, her sister:

> I grew up very, very isolated. My sister and brother, we had nothing to do with each other, hardly, as little as you can have. We had nothing to do with each other. I had no friends growing up. I was painfully, painfully shy, and insecure and depressed. My sister was pretty mean to me, she was older, she would ridicule me, she would get her friends to gang up on me. I got picked on cause I was also a very tiny kid, I was short, but I was also pretty skinny, so I got picked on. I was bullied, you know. I couldn't defend myself. I, you know, I was one those really pathetic kids. I was just a miserable kid. It was a very, very difficult time for me growing up. I was very, very shy and insecure. I was always depressed, I was always depressed. I was so unhappy. I was very suicidal throughout periods of my life really. I was looking at myself in the mirror and just feeling like, really just not wanting to be alive. There has always been a huge, a huge void in my life.

Rivka continued to expand on her use of alcohol: "I had gone through so many periods of my life not having any social contact, feeling no social connection. I think drinking made me feel socially connected while I was drunk."

The Preexperimental Self phases of these women were filled with significant problems. Participants' definitions of who they were at this time were affected by familial experiences. A sense of abandonment and/or isolation within family environments due to child sexual and/or physical abuse, as well as family violence experienced by mothers, affected the lives of thirteen participants. These participants seemingly did not have any outside supports at the time that could have made a difference in their self-evaluations. Often, participants did not have friends to turn to, nor were there significant others with whom women could experience themselves differently than they did in this phase.

For the remaining six participants, experiences of poor or insufficient parenting, feelings of isolation and/or abandonment, body image, and other traumatic events affected their self-images, signifying abuse and neglect as well. Therefore, it is not difficult to understand why they had trouble seeing themselves in a positive light in relation to families.

In *The Preexperimental Self* phase, nineteen participants were living in families who had negative ties to others in their social environments. The pattern generated here is twofold: (1) a similarity in participants' social backgrounds and experiences and (2) a similarity in how participants internalized these feelings of negative self-worth. The characteristics generated from these women's narratives were negative social connections with significant others in familial environments. It was very painful for participants to feel unable to initiate any actions for themselves. Families of origin led women to have feelings of shame, self-hate, depression, and low self-esteem, which crippled overall behaviors in *The Preexperimental Self* phase.

Social behavior develops as one responds to the expectations of others, as one experiences their norms, and through the process of social interaction as one anticipates the responses of others and then incorporates these responses into conduct patterns.[28] Research on women's experiences in the addiction/recovery field suggests that alcoholic and drug-dependent women suffer from lower self-esteem, more anxiety, and a greater sense of powerlessness and inadequacy than do men.[29] Other studies consider high rates of incest and other forms of early sexual and family violence among drug-dependent women.[30] Further, similar studies focus on women's experiences of violence and abusive relationships, leading in some cases to psychological problems such as conflict and powerlessness.[31] As Gannon argues, "Addictions are the first cousins in the family tree of child abuse."[32]

Certain social conditions set the phase for women to become addicted to alcohol and/or drugs either in the teenage years or in adulthood, leading to extremely negative self-evaluations. As highlighted in the following section, participants needed to deal with such feelings; therefore, this group of women began to experiment with alcohol and/or drugs.

The Experimental Self

> I used as it helped me deal with the pain I was experiencing. I didn't just want to feel any pain. I think it was just from all the trauma and stuff like that I dealt with and I didn't know how to deal with it. And it just, and I think I just didn't want to feel anything. (Marie)

In the preceding section, I highlighted how most participants had negative feelings toward their preexperimental selves due to varying family environments. Whether it was through family violence or a sense of abandonment, most participants had internalized feelings of low self-esteem, shame, and self-hate.

Negative social connections had shaped the women's sense of selves in *The Preexperimental Self* phase. Participants had made meanings of themselves according to how they saw themselves in relationship to significant others. The women were experiencing a "social reality"[33] that was being shaped by meanings they gave to these realities.

Marie's comment above clarifies the purpose of this section: to understand how participants began to experiment with alcohol and/or drugs in order to help them deal with meanings of these self-images and how this activity helped them to manage problems in their lives. Substances were the means by which participants attempted to regain a positive sense of self and a sense of control over a negative life.

As Marie noted above, "I just didn't want to feel anything." Her use of alcohol stemmed from the "trauma and stuff" she experienced in her family at the time of her experimentation. Eventually, she became addicted and stated that the alcohol managed to "work as I was overwhelmed with problems." Participants who eventually found that alcohol and/or drugs were helping them manage or cope with problems in their lives finally had discovered something that "worked" for them. They cited depression, anxiety, and low self-esteem as important factors pushing them into abusive alcohol and/or drug-using patterns. Substances were now helping them mask and obliterate negative feelings they had about themselves.

Although, in many instances, participants like Marie began to experiment because alcohol and/or drugs helped them cope with problems, others characterized their entry into such a lifestyle as a time of fun. Their reasons for experimentation were to satisfy their curiosity, to take risks, and to "fit in" with peers: in other words, to try it out.

Addiction happens over a period of time and is a rather slow process at the beginning.[34] Participants did not set out to become addicted, but, over a period of time, prolonged experimentation opened the door to extended usage of alcohol and/or drugs. Once they had become seasoned users, habits had been established. One participant, Shirley, found that, after her father had died, alcohol "eased the pain" of his death, and, as she stated, "I didn't hurt so much anymore." As with other participants, over time, her experimentation escalated into use.

Participants' introduction to substances was initiated through various influences: parents, siblings, peers, and/or boyfriends. The contexts of alcohol and drug experimentation for most women consisted of social groups with peers and/or siblings. For some participants, drugs commonly were available at school. For example, Susan commented that "[i]t wasn't that hard. In the school I was in it was all over the place. I mean everybody used. We had so many kids get busted."

One woman's experimentation was deliberate. As Martha explained, her experimental self phase involved using alcohol in order to manage sleeping problems due to family troubles, part of which was dealing with her abusive husband: "I started drinking a magnum over the weekend and I could sleep."

She eventually found that this use of alcohol "worked" for her in managing her life and, as a result, she continued on into her addiction.

Not only were some of the women experimenting out of curiosity and conformity—in order to be like peers and/or siblings—but also some deliberately began to use substances in order to cope with problems in their lives. I document two emergent characteristics that deal with participants' experimental self phases: (1) conformity and curiosity were common factors for thirteen participants in this phase, and (2) ten participants used alcohol and/or drugs as a coping mechanism.

Through experimentation, participants who were imitating peers' and/or siblings' use of alcohol and/or drugs were internalizing images that were congruent with those they admired. They were behaving in ways that made them similar to siblings and/or peers. They also were learning to attach meanings to their association with alcohol and/or drugs—participants were giving such substances a particular object status. At this time, through experimentation, these women were using substances as a means to an end—being part of the lives of significant others, "being part of the crowd," and "being part of the fun"—all important issues in young peoples' lives. Participants who used substances as a coping mechanism stated that their experimentation was intentional and that this action helped them to obliterate or bury images of negative selves. The following table highlights women's reasons for experimenting with alcohol and/or drugs.

Table 2.3. Women's Reasons for Experimenting with Alcohol and/or Drugs

Reasons	Frequency Percent	(n)
Conformity/Curiosity	52.0	(13)
Coping mechanism	40.0	(10)
Family usage	8.0	(2)
Total:	100.0	(25)

For thirteen participants, their use was to conform to significant others: peers, siblings, friends, and/or boyfriends. Ten women were using substances in order to cope or manage personal problems. For two participants, their use related to family usage, whereby women's families introduced them to alcohol and/or drugs.

Reasons for Using: Conformity and Curiosity

For thirteen participants, wanting to "fit in" was a salient factor and a very influential one through which they were introduced to alcohol and/or drugs in their younger years. For example, when I asked Susan why she started using, she commented that "[i]t just looked like they were all having fun and I just wanted to be part of that." Deb also stated that her drug use began through her experimentation with a group to which she wanted to belong:

> I was a freshman in high school. Started out more kind of like experimental, you know, most of my friends were a little bit older, so they were, um, drinking. Yeah, you know, that, the people that I was hanging around, which a lot of them were my, my sister was two years older than I was, and a lot of them were friends of hers also. Um, so that's the kind of crowd I got into. I wanted to do the same things that they did.

For Nancy, her early alcohol use was related to her "bunch of friends": "Well, I didn't drink every day, you know, because I was thirteen. But like once every three or four months, I would find a bunch of my friends and we'd go out and find somebody to buy us beer or wine or something, you know." Nancy related how, during this time, it was through her "parent's stash" of alcohol that she managed to continue using:

> Well, my parents, they drink scotch and I was babysitting my two younger sisters. My parents went out and I said, I've got to try this stuff, you know. They would have their cocktail every night after my Dad would get home from work. So I've got to see what this is like, you know. So they were out and I went and got the stuff. So it was my parent's stash.

For Betty, experimentation began with a crowd of friends as well: "I only used when I got with people that did it. I smoked pot, marijuana, a little bit of beer with them. And they had a problem, a drug problem, and when I would get with them, I would start doing it just like them, you know, being with the crowd."

Participants who began to use with peers were already in a social group of young people, and they wished to cement their belonging by doing the same things their group was doing, that is, using alcohol and/or drugs. Many participants believed that their social identities depended on it; it was a "cool" thing to do in their social groups.

Research on alcohol and drug addiction focuses on preexistent motives as a rationale for experimentation with substances. Research studies indicate that motives such as instant achievement, psychological support, imitation, thrill-seeking, relaxation, recreation, and a sense of well-being characterize the experimenter's frame of mind upon first usage of alcohol and/or drugs.[35] Other researchers argue that initiation into alcohol and/or drug use is a social process and needs to be analyzed in this light.[36] Blumer et al. argue against the notion of preexistent motives:

> It should be evident that induction into juvenile drug use is a complex social process. . . . [O]ne must view the recruitment of youngsters into drug use in the group context in which such recruitment actually goes on, and recognize that such recruitment is fundamentally a matter of being able to move into an already existing world and structure of drug use.[37]

Many researchers agree with Blumer et al.[38] that initial use of alcohol and/or drug use is social, that individuals may try it out of curiosity,[39] and that others may try it as it is a "cool" thing to do.[40]

Although many participants experimented because of peers' and siblings' influences, a few of the women talked about how they were also allowed to use substances with their parents' consent. Pat commented on how her mother enabled her use:

> Well, first my brothers and sisters, my older brothers and sisters were teenagers, and I knew all the time that they drank down in the basement, so I knew where to get it. And so that summer I hung out with the big kids and started getting into like smoking and that kind of thing. I started using because that was just a grown up thing. My mum, my mum was either in denial or she was just sheltered somehow, you know, by grace. She knew that we partied and she actually let us, she told us that if we would stay, we were the last of all the kids [ten siblings], if we would stay in school, then we could smoke pot in the house. So, we were allowed to smoke pot upstairs.

For other participants, their experimentation was due to curiosity. For example, Lynn noted:

> I started using drugs when I was about fourteen and drinking. I remember drinking when I was very young. First, sips out of my Dad's beer and then I would take the whole beer and put it in my closet and drink one a night. Even as a little kid, I had gone in and taken the alcohol and put back water until it was all gone. My parents both worked, so, a lot of time, we were home alone a lot.

Grace's early drug use began with her brothers, whom she greatly admired. Her brothers, who were much older, were using marijuana and introduced her to it at the age of ten. When I asked how she got the money to buy marijuana, she said: "My brothers worked. I'd get it through my brothers. My brothers worked and they would buy it and then they'd hook me onto it and get me high. And they would roll it for me." Grace expanded on the fact that she did not live with her parents at age ten, because one of her brothers had taken her in to live with him. When I asked why she lived with her brother instead of her parents, she stated: "Because by then he knew that I was addicted to marijuana and he knew that my mum and dad wouldn't approve of it. Which, they were alcoholics and they, they would drink and stuff; and that's how I kinda got by with it." Grace talked about her brothers many times throughout our interview, and I got the impression that they cared very much for her, as she did for them. Grace highlighted the fact that she continued to use as she got older, even though she knew it was the "wrong crowd" at the time: "Everybody else was doing it, and they said, 'Hey, it won't hurt you. Try it out,' you know. Me, being a kid, I said, 'Why not?'" She expanded on how this made her feel: "So I started smoking it [the marijuana]. And I liked the way it made me feel, at least that's what I thought. And then I was, as it went on, it started giving me bad headaches, but that didn't bother me. I still smoked it to get through the day."

Not all participants had positive experiences with first use. In fact, for a few women, their first time using was very unpleasant. For example, Shirley began to use at age thirteen. She highlighted this initial experience:

> I guess I had my first drink at about thirteen. My friend had a bottle of Southern Comfort. A brand new bottle of Southern Comfort and we each did a couple of shots. And that's all I remember and I woke up in the hospital because I almost killed myself 'cause I went back and drank the entire bottle of Southern Comfort. So that was my first experience with drinking. And my friend didn't do that; she stopped at a few shots. I didn't, I drank the entire bottle—and almost killed myself. That scared me for a few months, but it was just boom, I was just fast and furious from the get-go.

Although she had had such a negative experience with initial use, she ignored the effects and continued to use. She stated that she surrounded herself with what she termed "hard-core friends" and did not stop but, from then on, "always drank and always smoked pot."

For Betty, who earlier commented on using with "the crowd," the initial experience was also a negative one: "I partied with some friends and we did some kind of drug. I think it was called angel dust and it was a bomb and I got sick on it. I went into the bathroom, got on the floor and they had to call an ambulance, take me into the hospital and give me sedatives to calm me down." Despite this, she also continued to use substances for four years before she eventually quit.

The construction of positive attitudes toward alcohol and/or drugs after unpleasant experiences is explained in Becker's[41] work on becoming a marijuana user. Becker argues for the use of drugs for pleasure. First, if a person is to become a user, she must learn the proper technique: this is learned from other users. Second, the individual must believe that further usage will produce new experiences and continue to experiment with it until it does. With increasing experience of the drug, the user continues to learn to use the drug. Finally, the individual must learn to enjoy the effects she has learned to experience. In sum, a person cannot begin to use drugs for pleasure or continue to use them for pleasure, unless she learns to define their effects as enjoyable. The drug must become and remain an object that she has conceived of as capable of producing pleasure. Once there is a change in the user's conception of the drug occasioned by certain kinds of experiences with it, then the act of using becomes impossible. This change is seen in participants' actions in their recovery phases.

For one participant, Kathleen, the family environment was filled with "craziness" because her father had heart problems and he frequently forgot to take his nitroglycerine. Such events threw the rest of the family into chaos as they hurriedly "gave him his pills and his oxygen." Despite this, Kathleen was involved in gymnastics from age eleven to thirteen. Then her life began to change:

> I had fallen in with a crowd of, from the age of about eleven to thirteen; I was very involved in gymnastics. I did it every day; I taught gymnastics on Saturdays, and then I got, this was during the Vietnam War years, and started hanging out with a totally different kind of crowd like. A good friend whose father was the head of the young socialist alliance in [her home town] and I started going to antiwar demonstrations and I gave up on gymnastics around fourteen. I was the head cheerleader at our school and I just threw all that out. And I just went in a different direction and the giving up of like a goal and a dream.

Although Kathleen could not articulate specifically why she "gave up" and "went in a different direction," she did admit that this time "was very upsetting" to her and that she "started getting depressed." In continuing her story, Kathleen reiterated how

> [I] was always a risk-taker. I liked doing things that gave me an adrenaline rush. I can remember jumping off the roof of our garage. And always like when we would go to the symphonies, I'd always be imagining being like Spiderman. You know, so that was another part of it—that I liked the risk.

Kathleen suggested that she had a "genetic component" that contributed to her eventual addiction:

> I think that there was probably a genetic component cause the first time I ever picked up alcohol, I absolutely felt seduced, I felt a magnetic kind of attraction. Um, I didn't start out, um, dabbling with it. I mean I gulped, I never sipped. I always gulped, kind of um, literally and figuratively.

Several factors contributed to Kathleen's experimentation with substances: an upsetting family environment due to her father's illness, her risk-taking behavior, and her belief that "genetics" possibly played a part.

Two participants had no experimentation phase because they were introduced to the use of alcohol and/or drugs at a very young age through their primary socialization agents, that is, their parents. For these participants, their alcohol and/or drug use was normalized. For example, Mary explained that her initial taste of alcohol evolved from a particular tradition in the area where she grew up, one that was replicated for her when she was an infant. This tradition substantiated, for her, that the use of substances was normal within her household:

> It was pretty much as I understood it, an accepted procedure to give little infants liquor in the bottle to keep them asleep. I mean to cure colic or whatever, and it was a very general practice. I can remember my uncles taking a shot every morning and evening. It was for their heart, you know. It made them live longer, you know, so I just grew up around that. When I got to be about six years old, I figured I could

> ask for a little bit of beer or whatever. I tasted it and tried it around holidays.

She further expanded on how she felt about her taste for alcohol: "By the time I was nine, I was getting soused before Midnight Mass. I couldn't even go to church, because I was drinking crème de menthe. Yeah, and I'd put it on my ice cream." She continued by stating that, in high school, "I experimented with everything. I experimented with anything I could, you know, come across. I experimented with cocaine and hallucinogens in high school."

Sandy's socialization into addiction was with her family, who were all drug users and dealers. She noted that, because of this, she did not have any outside friends: "My family was all drug dealers. I never needed to go outside my family."

Many participants in this study (n=21) were exposed to drugs and alcohol while growing up within their families. Social learning theory has a clear-cut application in explaining their attraction to alcohol and/or drug use.[42] One major agent of socialization is tightly related to substance abuse: parents. In an individual's early years, parents who use legal drugs (i.e., alcohol, tobacco, and prescription drugs) are more likely to raise children who both drink and use illegal drugs than are parents who abstain completely. In other words, adolescents tend to internalize definitions and values and to engage in behavior "enacted and approved by significant others."[43] Obviously, participants' choices were influenced by socialization into a certain mode of coping with problems through seeing these actions taken by significant others in their early lives.

Events that together created these women's first-use situations included the opportunities to use, the availability of the substances, a willingness to experiment, and social milieus supportive of their use.[44] Most participants began alcohol and/or drug use in their early teens and eventually escalated their use principally because they found a number of benefits associated with substances. For some, these benefits came about within friendship networks, through emulating peers, or in order to feel normal with relevant significant others. They used substances for the meaning and value they derived from them; all participants found significance and meaning within the social contexts of alcohol and/or drug use.

Alcohol and/or drugs were particularly attractive for many women not only for the physiological effects they produced but also for the community and acceptance these women felt when with other users. For example, two participants were introduced to alcohol and drugs by their boyfriends. As Theresa explained:

> My first time, I did line after line [of cocaine] because I was kind of coerced into doing my first line, you know. You know, a boyfriend, of course. I did that first line and I'm like, okay, cut me up another one, and another. I was actually with a group that were suppliers and I dated one of them. I found out that they were dealing it. I mean I was sort of curious 'cause the guy I happened to be dating, he did it, and I started thinking, "Well, just one line. It's not going to hurt, I mean just one." Well, that one line was all it took for me.

For Lynn, her initiation was also with a boyfriend: "In high school, I was dating someone who was twenty-five, and we used to drink all the time. We'd smoke pot and do Quaaludes. We would do Black Beauties. It was actually a lot of fun."

From the foregoing discussion, it is evident that initiation phases for participants who began to experiment out of curiosity and/or to conform to significant others' behaviors, their experimentations were infrequent, and it was not a problem in their lives at this point.

The following discussion shows how two participants deliberately sought out substances in order to cope with negative self-images. The remainder of participants found that, through experimenting, alcohol and/or drugs were working and helping them manage feelings about themselves. What is relevant in this section is how participants talk about continuing experimentation with substances. They were finding that alcohol and/or drugs helped them deal with specific feelings they had at the time: unhappiness, social isolation, and low self-esteem.

Some Women's Reasons for Using: Coping

Two women who began to use substances in their later years (age thirty and up) did so deliberately in order to deal with problems. Linda had also used while in high school, and Martha had previously been a light social drinker. Linda began using alcohol at age thirty. She also stipulated that

> I remember drinking in high school—but that was just a one-time thing. But then I probably never drank until I was married, um, and then it was just occasions, birthdays, um, New Year's, you know, and maybe it wasn't even birthdays, because I was always pregnant too, I mean very pregnant. I had my first [child] at seventeen, then eighteen, nineteen, twenty-three, and twenty-five.

When I asked her to relate to me why she began to use seriously, she commented:

> I saw myself in a situation. The only reason I can think why, and I don't think it's a reason, but it's a fact that I had always been living with my parents or a husband, and when the second husband and I parted ways, that's when I started drinking. Not because of the parting, I don't think, it was because of the freedom. I would go out, by the time I was thirty, also my children were of an age that I was fairly free with my time, so, therefore, I could kind of, you know, socialize more with my peers.

Martha highlighted how her husband's behavior affected her and what she did in order to cope: "It was painful and one glass of wine didn't work anymore, so I had two. That helped me to sleep, or at least get to sleep. This went on for probably a year. It helped me sleep and that's what I was after."

In this particular phase, participants used words and descriptors that included: "It helped me deal with my depression, my low self-esteem"; "I felt in my mind that I had to have it every day to get me through my day"; "It gave me the energy to get through my day"; "I shut my emotions off [with the alcohol]"; "It helped me deal with the pain I was experiencing." For many participants, their alcohol and/or drug use was helping them cope with how they saw themselves at this time.

Hannah began to experiment along with her peers in high school; then, when she went to college, she "got into the party scene," where she was introduced to morphine, OxyContin, a variety of prescription drugs, and marijuana. Eventually, marijuana became her drug of choice. When I asked her to explain how her experimentation began, she commented:

> I have always dealt with low self-esteem, searching, trying to find an identity. I also had this, I don't know, I like adventure. I like to try new things, whatever, you know. So sure, I will give it a try. At that point, at that age, I didn't understand that it was a much deeper-rooted thing. I was trying to fulfill a need, a longing so I just started reaching out there for whatever came along to fill it up. Even though I didn't have a label, I didn't have a name for what that longing was, or for what that need was.

She understood that she had lost her sense of values. But she had also lost her best friend while in high school, and that loss further fueled her usage:

> I don't think, I don't think I really stuck to my morals that I grew up with, my values. When I was eighteen, I went against what was inside me deeply, what I knew between right and wrong, and I just discarded it and I thought, well, I know what feels good, you know, and it just sort of snowballed from there. I also had a loss of my best friend my senior year of high school. She died and that just sort of pushed me over the edge, you know, it was like I felt like I died the day she did, and then I refused to grieve. I shut it off.

Hannah continued by stating that she continued to use in order to "pretend like I wasn't hurting," masking the emotional pain she was experiencing and giving her a sense of safety from feelings of grief.

Rivka's experimentation was a short one. From a very early age, she had been training to be a dancer. When she was seventeen, she was riding her bicycle in the "back country fifty-mile loop and I got hit by a car." It took a long time for her to recover, and, when she did, she realized that she could no longer dance: she had a deformed leg from the accident. She realized while in recovery from the accident that "I couldn't dance anymore and that had really been the thing that had kept me going. 'Cause I just had a real passion for that and I had never really had a passion for anything else. So I was pretty miserable and always depressed [after the accident]." So, when given the opportunity with friends at a party, she began to drink in order

> [t]o feel better. I did it to feel better. I was extremely depressed and what happened was, I went to a party. I'd never had more than a few sips of alcohol and I got very, very drunk, and I felt very good. I got drunk very quickly. And it just totally alleviated my depression. I was very socially inept and I was interacting well with people [while drunk]. And from then on, I was getting drunk almost every night—it was like an overnight thing.

Esther had been bulimic and anorexic while in high school and college. She had never used drugs until she graduated from college at age twenty-five. While at a concert, she was introduced to Ecstasy by friends who encouraged her to try it. She prefaced this experience by stating, "Before that, I'd had very low self-esteem all my life. I was always self-conscious in public." Then she proceeded to talk about the drug's effects:

> As it started to hit me, it was the first time I've ever seen myself in a positive light. I can remember, I unfolded my arms. I felt all my self-consciousness leave my body, and I sat down for awhile and I just felt very reflective. Um, and I thought it was the best thing in the world.

Following this experience, she continued to use and, as she stated, "loved it every time."

As people get older, selective peer-group interaction and socialization comprise the single most powerful factor related to alcohol and/or drug use among individuals.[45] For participants, social learning was a mediating variable, which influenced the kind of choices participants were making. Imitation and social influences played significant roles in initiating and maintaining alcohol and/or drug use among participants. "Over time, participation in specific groups or social circles reinforces certain values and patterns of activity."[46] Participants were socialized into values favorable to alcohol and/or drug use by the social circles they interacted in and were involved with.[47] Therefore, use of substances can be explained by differential exposure to groups in which use is rewarded. As Akers et al. argue:

> These groups provide the social environments in which exposure to definitions, imitations of models, and social reinforcements for use of or abstinence from any particular substance take place. The definitions are learned through imitation and social reinforcement of them by members of the group with whom one is associated.[48]

As this section highlights, the use of alcohol and/or drugs within particular social environments—with families, siblings, peers, and/or boyfriends—shaped participants' sense of self. Other than the one participant, who was in a family of users and sellers, most seemed to be drifting into alcohol and/or drug use. They were not using constantly, nor did they see themselves as addicts; they were using on only an occasional basis with significant others. But, as other women made clear, their selection of substances was helping them deal with personal problems. Alcohol and/or drugs were helping them "to shut their emotions off" and to deal with the pain they were experiencing in their lives.

Participants already had experimented with various types of alcohol and/or drugs before they settled on their drug(s) of choice. These included stimulants such as cocaine, including crack, downers, and amphetamines ("speed"); hallucinogens, such as LSD ("acid"); Phencyclidine (PCP); MDMA (Ecstasy); marijuana; and psilocybin mushrooms. Narcotics, such as heroin, morphine, and OxyContin, were also favorites. Depressants included alcohol, Quaaludes, Valium, barbiturates, and tranquilizers/sedatives. Several participants had used analgesics, including Demerol, muscle relaxers, and various prescription drugs. Most participants had tried other drugs in their experimentation phases, but such drugs were, in many cases, not to their liking. For example, Deb tried acid at a concert and, as she stated, "It just sort of freaked me out, so I'm not doing this again." And Hannah, too, talked about how she "had started out with" alcohol, marijuana, and prescription drugs, but as she stated, "Marijuana was always the one I always had to have with me all the time. I always had to have it." Participants, then, over a period of time, eventually became "seasoned users"[49] with their alcohol and/or drug(s) of choice.

Whether women began experimenting with alcohol and/or drugs with friends, siblings, boyfriends, or peers, over a period of time their motivations for abusing substances shifted: they came to enjoy the effects of the substances, the tranquilizing effects, and euphoric feelings they gained from continuing alcohol and/or drug use. Sometimes it was even more. For example, a friend took Robbie to a bar for an evening out. Her initial use not only provided her with a sense of normalcy but also was the beginning of a love affair with her drug of choice, alcohol:

> She [a friend] took me to a bar and I fell in love. I thought it was the best place in the world, you know, and with a few drinks, I felt normal. I felt like I was the same as everybody else I saw. I could talk. I could laugh. I could dance. I could joke around. I could flirt a little bit. All those things that had confused me about how other people had managed to do them, I was able to do with a little bit of this [the alcohol], and I truly fell in love.

Whether participants occasionally used, or intentionally started to use, self-perceptions were beginning to change, that is, meanings toward themselves were beginning to alter. Experimentation was enabling them to see themselves in a different light. In this phase, alcohol and/or drugs were becoming the medium through which they began to change. Therefore, common characteristics in this phase of participants' lives showed that they were beginning to experience themselves differently. They were not yet "seasoned users,"[50] but, in their experimental phase, their habits, however mild, had been started.

Summary

In this chapter, I have highlighted two issues that were important at this point in participants' lives: (1) how they were making meanings of themselves in *The Preexperimental Self* phase within specific situations and family backgrounds and (2) how they were making meanings of themselves and their relationships to alcohol and/or drugs as they began to experiment with substances in *The Experimental Self* phase. Through women's narratives, I have considered the relevant characteristics of participants' sense of selves and social identities that existed during these phases. There is now a greater understanding of the influential factors that affected their lives, along with a better explanation of how they perceived themselves during this time. Women in this study were traveling different paths into their addictions and there were commonalties in their lives at this point. In chapter 3, I focus on how women experienced addictions in earnest and on how they managed and practiced ongoing addicted selves.

Notes

1. R. Granfield and W. Cloud, *Coming Clean: Overcoming Addiction without Treatment* (New York University Press, 1999), 59.

2. H. Blumer, *Symbolic Interactionism: Perspective and Method* (Englewood Cliffs, NJ: Prentice Hall, 1969).

3. Granfield and Cloud, *Coming Clean*, 59.

4. E. Goode, *Drugs in American Society,* fifth ed. (Boston: McGraw-Hill, 1999).

5. C. A. Faupel, G. Hortowitz, and G. Weaver, *The Sociology of American Drug Use* (Boston, MA: McGraw-Hill, 2004).

6. S. Brown, *Treating the Alcoholic: A Developmental Model of Recovery* (New York: John Wiley and Sons, 1985).

7. N. Denzin, *The Alcoholic Self* (Newbury Park, CA: Sage, 1987).

8. A. Giddens, *The Constitution of Society* (Cambridge, MA: Polity Press, 1984).

9. P. Cohen, "Cocaine Use in Amsterdam in Non-Deviant Subcultures" (paper presented at the International Council on Alcohol and Addictions Congress, Lausanne, Switzerland, June 1987).

10. J. Charon, *Symbolic Interactionism: An Introduction, an Interpretation, an Integration,* seventh ed. (Upper Saddle River, NJ: Prentice Hall, 2001); J. Hewitt, *Self and Society: A Symbolic Interactionist Social Psychology,* ninth ed. (Boston: Allyn and Bacon, 2003); K. Sandstrom, D. Martin, and G. Fine, *Symbols, Selves, and Social Reality: A Symbolic Interactionist Approach to Social Psychology and Sociology* (Los Angeles: Roxbury, 2003).

11. Sandstrom, Martin, and Fine, *Symbols, Selves, and Social Reality,* 12.

12. Sandstrom, Martin, and Fine, *Symbols, Selves, and Social Reality,* 12.

13. Charon, *Symbolic Interactionism*, 39.

14. H. Becker, B. Geer, E. Hughes, and A. Strauss, *Boys in White: Student Culture in Medical School* (Chicago: University of Chicago Press, 1992).

15. A. Lindesmith, A. Strauss, and N. Denzin, *Social Psychology* (New York: Holt, Rinehart, and Winston, 1977), 174.

16. N. Websdale, "Rural Woman Abuse: The Voices of Kentucky Women," in *De-*

viance and Deviants, An Anthology, ed. R. Tewksbury and P. Gagne (Los Angeles: CA: Roxbury Publishing Company, 2000), 163–73.

17. A. Bushy, *Proceedings from the National Rural Health Association Conference* (Center for Health Economics Research, 1993); W. DeKeseredy, M. D. Schwartz, D. Fagen, and M. Hall, "Separation/Divorce Sexual Assault: The Contribution of Male Support," *Feminist Criminology* (July 2006): 228–50; P. L. Gagne, "Appalachian Women: Violence and Social Control," *Journal of Contemporary Ethnography* 20 (1992): 387–415; Websdale, "Rural Woman Abuse," 163–73.

18. Websdale, "Rural Woman Abuse," 163–73.

19. L. Gorham, "The Growing Problem of Low Earnings in Rural Areas," in *Rural Poverty in America*, ed. C. Duncan (New York: Auburn House, 1992), 21–39.

20. Gagne, "Appalachian Women," 387–415.

21. Bushy, *Proceedings from the National Rural Health Association Conference;* Gagne, "Appalachian Women," 387–415.

22. Websdale, "Rural Woman Abuse," 163–73.

23. DeKeseredy, Schwartz, Fagen, and Hall, "Separation/Divorce Sexual Assault," 228–50.

24. J. Ussher, "A Feminist Perspective," in *Living with Drink: Women Who Live with Problem Drinkers*, ed. R. Velleman, A. Copello, and J. Maslin (London: Longman, 1998).

25. D. Kendall, *Sociology in Our Times: The Essentials*, fourth ed. (Belmont, CA: Wadsworth/Thomson Learning, 2004).

26. Kendall, *Sociology in Our Times.*

27. A. Sev'er, *Fleeing the House of Horrors: Women Who Have Left Abusive Partners* (Toronto, Ontario, Canada: University of Toronto Press, 2002), 19.

28. R. Stephens, *The Street Addict Role: A Theory of Heroin Addiction* (Albany: State University of New York Press, 1991).

29. L. Beckman, "Self-Esteem of Women Alcoholics," *Journal of Studies on Alcohol* 39, no. 3 (1978): 491–98; E. Ettorre, *Women and Substance Use* (London: Macmillan, 1992).

30. L. Blood and A. Cornwall, "Childhood Sexual Victimization as a Factor in the Treatment of Substance Misusing Adolescents," *Substance Use and Misuse* 31, no. 8 (1996): 1015–39; B. A. Miller and W. R. Downs, "The Impact of Family Violence on the Use of Alcohol by Women," *Alcohol Health and Research World* 17 (1993): 137–43; P. Raine, *Women's Perspectives on Drugs and Alcohol: The Vicious Circle* (Hampshire, England: Ashgate, 2001); V. Ryan and J. Popour, "Five-Year Women's Plan," Capitol Area Substance Use Commission, for the Office of Substance Use (OSAS), Michigan Department of Health, IV, 4c, IV, 12c, 1983.

31. J. P. Gannon, *Soul Survivors: A New Beginning for Adults Abused as Children* (New York: Prentice Hall, 1989), 116.

32. Gannon, *Soul Survivors,* 116.

33. Sandstrom, Martin, and Fine, *Symbols, Selves, and Social Reality,* 12.

34. S. Brown, *Treating the Alcoholic: A Developmental Model of Recovery* (New York: John Wiley and Sons, 1985); M. Rosenbaum, *Women on Heroin* (New Brunswick, NJ: Rutgers University Press, 1981).

35. A. Y. Cohen, "Inside What's Happening: Sociological, Psychological, and Spiritual Perspectives on the Contemporary Drug Scene," *American Journal of Public Health* 59 (1969): 2092–95; D. J. Feldman and H. S. Feldman, "On the Etiology of Narcotic Addiction and Its Relation to Curiosity," *Psychosomatics* 13 (1972): 304–8; M. Keeler, "Motivation for Marijuana Use: A Correlate of Adverse Reactions," *American Journal of Psychiatry* 125 (1968): 142–46; G. L. Minzner, J. T. Barker, and P. H. Werme, "Patterns of Drug Use among College Students: A Preliminary Report," *American Journal of Psy-*

chiatry 127 (1970): 15–24.

36. R. L. Coombs, J. Fry, and P. G. Lewis, eds., *Socialization in Drug Use* (Cambridge, MA: Schenkman, 1976); Rosenbaum, *Women on Heroin,* 35.

37. H. Blumer, A. Sutter, R. Smith, and S. Ahmed, *The World of Youthful Drug Use* (Berkeley: Regents of the University of California, 1967), 173.

38. Blumer, Sutter, Smith, and Ahmed, *World of Youthful Drug Use,* 173.

39. B. S. Brown, S. K. Gauvey, M. B. Myers, and S. D. Stark, "In Their Own Words: Addicts' Reasons for Initiating and Withdrawing from Heroin," *International Journal of the Addictions* 6 (1971): 635–45.

40. H. Feldman, "Ideological Supports to Becoming and Remaining a Heroin Addict," *Journal of Health and Social Behavior* 9 (1968): 131–39; Rosenbaum, *Women on Heroin,* 35.

41. H. Becker, "Becoming a Marijuana User," *American Journal of Sociology* 59 (1953): 235–42.

42. Goode, *Drugs in American Society,* 109.

43. Goode, *Drugs in American Society,* 109.

44. Granfield and Cloud, *Coming Clean,* 59.

45. D. Kandel, "Inter-Generational and Intragenerational Influences on Adolescent Marijuana Use," *Journal of Social Issues* 30, no. 2 (1974): 197–35.

46. Goode, *Drugs in American Society,* 109.

47. Goode, *Drugs in American Society,* 109.

48. R. M. Akers, M. Kron, L. Lanza-Kaduse, and M. Radosevich, "Social Learning and Deviant Behavior: A Specific Test of a General Theory," *American Sociological Review* 44 (1979): 638.

49. Rosenbaum, *Women on Heroin,* 35.

50. Rosenbaum, *Women on Heroin,* 35.

Chapter 3

The Addicted Self

Introduction

> And I mean it was so wonderful just to do that [go to a bar for the first time], and it was like it had taken all that stress away and fitting in which was just such a wonderful feeling. Bridging that whole gap that had always been because for me as a victim, it was all about that there was something wrong with me. It was not them, it was me. If I had been better, if I had been right, if I had done this, if I had done that, then it wouldn't be like this. For me, I know I have talked with a lot of women in recovery and a lot of them drank to cover up the pain, to make the pain go away but I didn't. I drank to feel normal. I drank to fit in, not to fit in with them, but to fit in for me, so it would like calm all those worries, all those feelings of inadequacy and being different, all that stuff was just calmed with it. It was great. (Robbie)

Chapter 2 illustrated how women were making meanings toward themselves and toward alcohol and/or drugs in *The Preaddicted Self* phase and how participants' preaddicted selves had been shaped through various situations and circumstances that affected their self-images. Through the medium of alcohol and/or drug experimentation, these women were beginning to see themselves in a different light; thus, they were beginning to experience themselves differently.

This chapter is divided into three sections: (1) *The Pleasurable Self,* which highlights the fun and sense of security participants felt within alcohol and/or drug culture, (2) *The Immersed Drug Self,* which shows how central addiction was to participants' lives, and (3) *The Disgusted Self,* which considers how women began to rethink how they felt about themselves as addicts. In this chapter, I survey how participants saw their alcohol and/or drug selves, significant others in their lives, and the substances they were using as they experienced addiction—in other words, how participants were managing their addicted selves. Robbie, who experienced sexual abuse in her childhood beginning at the age of six, highlights the overall theme in this chapter when she states: "I drank to fit in, not to fit in with them, but to fit in for me." Her statement mirrors the narratives of other participants as they talk about how alcohol and/or drugs of choice were helping them to deal with feelings about themselves in addicted phases.

The purpose of this section is to explore and highlight how participants' use of alcohol and/or drugs provided them with another sense of self, both personal and social. Obviously, their use of substances in this phase influenced their lives, self-concepts, and actions. For twenty-three participants, the use of alcohol and/or drugs did not take place in a vacuum; women were relating to reference groups that provided them with other images or self-concepts that were of value to them. As Shibutani argues: "A self-concept consists of a set of beliefs and presuppositions . . . . [about oneself as an object and] is the product of participation in a long succession of social transactions."[1]

A reference group is that group whose outlook is used as a frame of reference for making judgments and decisions.[2] "The view of the reference group we relate to the most acts as a lens through which we see the world."[3] Self-concepts can change as one has new experiences; such revisions generally occur when individuals become involved with new groups or begin participating in different activities.[4] For example, participants told me about seeing themselves differently and about how the changing directions of their lives related to developing new reference groups. They were, as Shibutani[5] argues, displacing one reference group with another. This displacement involved a loss of responsiveness to the demands of one social world and the adoption of the perspectives of another. Often participants not only were developing new relationships and self-concepts that either excluded or depreciated their old values, but they also were avoiding former significant others, that is, families, partners, children, and previous reference groups, such as churches.

Through involvement with alcohol and/or drugs, participants experienced other selves. During *The Pleasurable Self* phase, substances provided participants with much pleasure and a sense of security within a community of other users who seemingly cared for them. Robbie highlighted these points as she told me about her bar experiences: "I found jobs there [at the bar]. I mean those people took care of me. It was the only time in my life that I ever had a surprise birthday party that people at a bar gave me. I mean it was my family, better than my family and for a long, long time, that was the greatest place."

Many of the women forged what one called "druggie" identities that helped them manage unhappy, imperfect lives for a time, ranging from six months to twenty-four years. For example, as Rivka noted, "I was so unhappy and the only thing that made me happy was alcohol." But, as their addictions progressed and they experienced "druggie" selves, disgusted selves began to emerge. As Kathleen noted, "I was at the point that I couldn't stand being inside myself any longer. You know, I could not stand to be inside of me." They began to interpret and define their relationships to alcohol and/or drugs in a different light; substances were no longer working for them. Eventually, they came to dislike their addicted selves intensely.

The following section begins with an overview of participants' primary substance of choice, the ages when they began addiction, and their experiences of the addictive phases.

Women's Drug(s) of Choice

The term *drug(s) of choice* refers here to the substance that participants identified as their primary or favorite drug: the one that they used regularly or the one that they were recovering from. Table 3.1 shows the distribution of participants' alcohol and/or drug(s) of choice as they entered addictive phases.

Table 3.1. Participants' Primary Drug(s) of Choice

Drug(s)	Frequency percent	(n)
Alcohol	52.0	(13)
Alcohol/Marijuana	28.0	(7)
Marijuana	4.0	(1)
Cocaine	8.0	(2)
Prescription drug (Darvocet)	4.0	(1)
Other (Ecstasy)	4.0	(1)
Total:	100.0	(25)

The primary substance of choice for thirteen participants was alcohol. Alcohol and marijuana were the drugs of choice for seven participants, while one woman was using only marijuana regularly. The remaining participants varied in their singular use of cocaine (n=2), the prescription drug Darvocet (n=1), and Ecstasy (n=1).

Ages at Which Women Became Addicted

One of the first questions I asked participants in the interviews was at what ages they became addicted. What I found interesting and somewhat surprising in these discussions was that they all knew when alcohol and/or drugs became an important part of their lives. Even though many of the women were looking back over a period of years, participants knew almost exactly at what ages they became addicted. These were eventful and salient experiences in their lives, ones that influenced their futures in many ways.

Most participants became addicted during their teenage years. The following table highlights the ages when women self-reported that addictive careers began in earnest.

One woman began using marijuana at the very early age of five; seven of the participants were between the ages of ten and fifteen when they began initial use; and eleven were between the ages of sixteen and twenty. Well over half of these participants began regular use as they entered their teens or while they were in their teen years. Three participants began using between the ages of twenty-one and thirty, while the remaining women (n=3) were more than thirty years of age when they began their initial use.

Table 3.2. Ages at Which Women Became Addicted

Age	Frequency percent	(n)
<10	4.0	(1)
10–15	28.0	7)
16–20	44.0	(11)
21–25	4.0	(1)
26–30	8.0	(2)
>30	12.0	(3)
Total:	100.0	(25)

Countless studies on the use of substances have shown that the principal motivating factor underlying "turning on" to alcohol and/or drugs in one's teenage years is that one's friends use such substances.[6] Young people gravitate toward those who are compatible with them in behavior, values, and personality. One of the strongest motivations for behavior among juveniles is the desire to gain and to maintain acceptance by their peers.[7] Various studies have found that alcohol and/or drug use among juveniles is social in nature and that peer influence is one of the most important factors.[8] So it is not unusual that this group of women also used along with teenage friends.

Data released in a new national study on alcohol and/or drug use among girls and women in the United States[9] and Canada[10] indicate that substance use is an increasingly significant problem that is starting earlier and earlier in girls' lives. For example, the report shows that the use of alcohol and marijuana for girls has changed. In the early 1960s, about 7 percent of new users of alcohol were between the ages of ten and fourteen; by the early 1990s, that percentage had increased to 31 percent. Similarly, marijuana use by young girls had also increased from 5 percent in the 1960s to a high of 24 percent in the 1990s. Overall, data[11] indicate that girls have caught up with boys in illicit drug and alcohol use and have actually surpassed boys in cigarette and prescription drug use. There are also more girls than boys who are new users of substances. The findings show that when girls use illicit drugs, marijuana is the most commonly used substance.

Overall, the rate of marijuana use, especially among rural adolescents, is only slightly lower than rates of use among urban youth. Usage rates for certain hard drugs, including inhalants and stimulants, are higher for rural youth, but tranquilizer use shows no rural-urban differences. However, urban youth still exhibit higher usage rates for cocaine and cocaine derivatives, heroin, and LSD.[12] For the last two years that research is available (2003–2004), more teenage girls than boys started using marijuana, alcohol, and cigarettes.[13]

The purpose of this first section is to explore participants' pleasurable selves as they became users. Initially, most women liked the "highs" they were experiencing along with feelings of relaxation and freedom from worry.

The Pleasurable Self

> I did a lot of drugs, a lot of drugs and I loved it. I felt great and I had a good time. Yeah, I used for years, a smorgasbord of drugs. I loved it. It was the greatest thing. (Shirley)

In this section, I explore how participants felt about themselves as they began addiction in earnest. Entry into addiction seemed to them to have positive functions. They reported that alcohol and/or drugs were causing them to feel more social, that they were stress relievers, and that they were making them happy and helping them to obliterate hurting selves. Alcohol and/or drug use gave them more energy, relief from discomfort, feelings of safety, and more introspection. Substances were their best friends, helping them to escape from reality, to become more aware, and to "feel awake." Alcohol and/or drugs were life-changing and helped them finally to feel, as many participants state, "okay."

As participants became addicted, *The Pleasurable Self* phase offered them other sources of meaning, a way of coping with life and artificially attaining feelings and rewards[14] that they believed they could not achieve in any other way. For many, addiction to alcohol and/or drugs followed a perceived need to transcend normal states and to give them meaningful relationships that eluded them in the "straight world."

As illustrated by the quotes discussed below, participants began to slip into dependency as their selves began to change. They were not denying problems in this phase; they simply did not define experiences in addictive phases as problematic. In this phase, no negative aspects of addiction impinged in any meaningful way on their lives.

The following three characteristics emerged in *The Pleasurable Self* phase: (1) For twenty-two participants, immersion in an alcohol and/or drug culture depended on the availability of substances and the opportunity to use with significant others. (2) For these women, usage was tied to activities in an alcohol and/or drug culture that generated pleasure and fun. (3) A sense of self-estrangement was common among all participants. The opportunity to use substances that participants discuss in the quotes below show how they eventually were no longer experimenting but were becoming immersed in an alcohol and/or drug culture. Participants began to leave customary behaviors behind. They began to associate with other alcohol and/or drug users in their lives and finally became "seasoned users."[15]

A major indicator in this phase was the dominant feelings participants had toward significant others and toward themselves as they became immersed in an alcohol and/or drug culture. In this phase, nineteen participants who had experienced family violence and/or a sense of isolation within social contexts related to significant others within an alcohol and/or drug culture that allowed them to feel socially connected. Alcohol and/or drug use provided them with opportunities to experience themselves differently. It is ironic that through substance use they became connected to themselves in a positive way.

Common descriptors for participants in this phase included, among other comments, "enjoying being part of the drug crowd," "being a party animal," "drugs mellowed me out," and "I liked the rush." Participants who began to experiment due to peer pressure were availing themselves of the opportunity to use with like-minded others who were meaningful to them. Although they originally had experimented out of conformity and/or curiosity, they soon became immersed in an alcohol and/or drug culture that was becoming important in their lives. The social contexts in which participants were becoming immersed framed their interpretations of themselves within such a culture; they were becoming socially committed as alcoholics and/or drug addicts. For participants, their entries into addiction were providing positive functions for them.

Women's Opportunity to Use with Significant Others

For all but three participants (who used in isolation), continued use of alcohol and/or drugs revolved around significant others at the time they became immersed in this culture. Deb's experiences often were with her boyfriends: "It depended on whom I was with at the time." Many times, her relationships with other users involved her "staying up all night partying, you know." What was important for Deb was the social context in which she used, with like-minded others: "I was not one to stay home and drink, you know, that was kind of part of the enjoyment for me is just getting intoxicated with other people."

For Rhonda, significant others were also important: she noted that she often used with a boyfriend "who was also a user." When I asked Rhonda to explain to me how alcohol made her feel, she explained: "I was kind of a loner always—a misfit, and I felt that when I drank, all my inhibitions came out, and I felt better."

And Mary, whose initial experimentation took place in her hometown, eventually moved to New York and met someone whom she "fell in love with," and there she continued by becoming immersed into drug culture:

> But then when I got into New York City, the crack was really prevalent. I met someone who was super addicted and ran his life around trying to get it and I thought I was in love with him, so I ran my life around him. I fell into the drug crowd and I, you know, that was perfect for me, hey, you know.

She continued by talking about how her usage "[k]ind of lifted me out of my world and having to think about having to deal with my problems. I felt cool, I felt like I was in with all the crowd. I was like the party animal. I was the one."

Grace also expanded her addiction with other users, when they would "use" people in order to get drinks: "Sometimes, if I didn't have the money, I'd go with my friends and me and my friends would use friends, or use people to get drinks, to get our drinks. You know, we used to use people. And, then, we used to go out and dance."

Esther, who was addicted to Ecstasy and manufactured it during her addictive phase, talked about how she used with a friend. Although she characterized their actions as "stupid stuff," it was fun and a social time for her:

> I was at my friend's house. And she had a country cabin. I would always spend the night there quite frequently, ah, we would go hiking, do whatever. We'd do a lot of Ecstasy together actually. Um, one of the things we'd like to do was eat Ecstasy and go on night hikes, and so we'd like, you know, spotlight owls and look at the birds that we could see, like night birds and things that we came across. She had an old barn on her property, so we'd play in the hay and stupid stuff.

For Kathleen, "home away from home was bars": "I'm telling you I spent a lot of time in bars, lots of time. I'd go to bars at 2:30 in the afternoon and leave at 2:30 in the morning."

As the above quotes illustrate, most participants' alcohol and/or drug use took place with significant others who obviously gave meanings to their use of substances within particular social contexts. For example, Theresa said that she immersed herself with other users, thus enabling her addiction. Often, it was not enough just to have using friends. Theresa's friends reinforced, through their use of the "pure" drug, the notion that at the time, it was "the right crowd" for her:

> I got into the wrong crowd. But for what I was doing, it was the right crowd. There was a bunch of coke-dealing Mexicans, most of them. Most of them didn't go to high school. I'm pretty sure most of them were illegals living outside of our town, but they actually went down to Mexico and they actually brought it back. I mean I've seen like bags, packed with bags like the size of your pillow of it. Yeah, that's where, and I think my addiction was, I mean I think it was a lot worse than it would have been if I had been hanging out with someone else because then they probably would have been getting it from them, but since I was actually with that group, I was getting more the pure cocaine than, you know. They usually split it up to where most of it's like baking powder or baking soda. Not quite as much coke, but I was getting the majority of the coke.

Twenty-two participants found that their use with other alcohol and/or drug users provided positive functions for them, that is, fun and pleasure were salient features of their using.

Addiction—A Sense of Pleasure and Fun

Participants signify that pleasure and fun were important aspects of their alcohol and/or drug use and figure prominently in the following quotes. As the women related, use of substances gradually seduced them into a committed use. I heard many participants in this phase state that alcohol and/or drug use made them feel "euphoric." Other descriptors included the words "mellow," "energetic," "happy," "fun," "celebrating," "easy," and "love."

As participants described how they felt about their alcohol and/or drug use the way they talked—even their body language—changed. They moved around and got very excited; their enthusiasm was palpable as they told me about how substances made them feel when they were addicted. It was an obvious delight for them even to tell me about their feelings as they related experiences from their addictive phases. Participants were vivid in their recollections. For example, Fran stated that, "[i]t just made me mellow out. That's what I felt like. I would take two or three of them [Darvocet] and I felt like I was on a year's drunk." Ann concurred as she said, "It mellowed me out. If I got drunk, you know, so I wouldn't have to worry about nothing, you know."

Hannah experienced feelings of euphoria: "Yeah, I mean it's just like ohhhhhhhh. You have the energy, you can do, you know, and you just feel good, that euphoric feeling." Rhonda's use had a double role. She used it as a crutch to "get rid of some things," and it also provided her with feelings of euphoria: "It felt good. At first, it could be that euphoric." Rivka claimed that "I was so unhappy and the only thing that made me happy was alcohol. I was a very happy and fun drunk." Pat talked about how "happy" her use made her feel as well as "just kind of hippy like and colorful and, you know, just celebrating life, and I was just like incredibly happy."

For most participants, the pleasure and fun they experienced as they entered their addictive phases were hard to resist. For Theresa, the use of cocaine made her feel more talkative and more awake: "I liked the rush, the adrenaline rush kept me up and moving and talkative. Yeah, it was pretty good for awhile."

Although Esther used infrequently with her boyfriend, it was "very fun, very fun" when she did:

> There were times when we would do it, very fun, very fun. I mean being the self-conscious person is the time you really would want to take your clothes off and just dance, and we would dance around, light the candles, play our favorite songs, sit Indian style, hold each other's hands, just tell each other how much we loved each other. It's a very easy drug.

For Grace, who was addicted to what she called, "the hard stuff," her feelings were positive in her addictive phase: "I liked the hard stuff, whiskey, gin, Jack Daniels, Southern Comfort. Ah, Black Velvet, you name it, I drank it. Oh, I loved it."

Overall, the addictive phase made most participants feel more comfortable with themselves. Probably Lynn said it best: "It's something that we do because we can't figure out what's wrong with us and we never fit in." She explained further, "I didn't feel like I fit in until I drank. I didn't feel like I was okay until I drank or did drugs. So, you don't feel like you're okay."

It is not difficult to understand that in this phase participants liked or "loved" their experiences. They were in the honeymoon period of addiction.

Alcohol and/or drug experiences had become meaningful, satisfying, pleasing, enjoyable, and self-reinforcing. The honeymoon phase, also called a "pink cloud,"[16] is characterized by elation, pleasure, high self-esteem, and denial of other problems.

Alcohol and/or drugs were the social objects that provided participants with effective solutions to their problems or troubles, as well as fun and pleasure with like-minded others. They had constructed a social world composed almost exclusively of other addicts; they had become "inundated"[17] in drug culture whereby their concerns were now pivoting around a single, all-informing identity.[18]

In this social world, there were as yet no consequences to using. Lynn stated it well when she said, referring to her use of alcohol, "That was my life; that was my whole life."

The following section provides insights into how women were now starting to feel as they experienced alcohol and/or drug use. As their quotes illustrate, they found that addiction was providing them with something meaningful in their lives—estrangement from initial selves.

Women's Sense of Self-Estrangement

Although three participants used in isolation, the remaining participants (n=22) in addictive phases followed a pattern of relating to reference groups that were congruent with their desired self-image. As the women talked about this phase, what emerged from the analysis was a wish to change their personalities in order to manage the discomfort of dealing with "people," and "the world." All twenty-five participants indicated that they needed a "release" from how they felt about themselves at this point. Many stressed how important it was for them to find a safe place away from negative self-images. Twenty-two participants had constructed and created meanings of value within a social context of addiction. For three participants, this safe place was not with others: they had used alcohol and/or drugs in isolation. Substances had become social objects through which participants came to like themselves.

For example, Mary talked about how her drugs of choice—alcohol, crack, and cocaine—helped her in dealing with herself in this phase: "I didn't have to be accountable to that person [meaning herself]." Nor did she have "to care" about that person. Her usage gave her another identity, one that she did not need to claim as a part of herself. Nor did she need to be accountable at all for her actions:

> It, I guess, it kind of lifted me out of my world, it gave me a release from the world and having to think about having to deal with my problems. It gave me like a temporary, you know, having to think about and worry about things or whatever. It gave me the chance to act like a different person and find a personality for me, be rude, be mean. But, then, you know, when the effects wore off, I didn't have to be accountable to that person. I didn't have to, you know, I didn't

> have to have people look at me and say, "Oh, there's that girl that was acting all crazy, laughing and funny and wild." I was just back to, to the person who didn't know, didn't care to know about themselves.

It was obvious to Mary that her drugs of choice had now become the social objects that helped her to "act like a different person," lifting her into another world in which she could be problem-free. Mary's life had been difficult. She left her hometown and began to live in New York at age twenty-five, working as a prostitute and dealing with a pimp who constantly used her. During this time she had three babies by caesarean section, one child by her pimp. So it was understandable when she said about her addicted self: "I had so many physical problems and I just felt like when I was high I didn't have to think about this stuff, you know, I was just out there having my fun and I was safe. I was in this whole, safe world."

Many other participants explained how alcohol and/or drug use helped them to escape their realities. As Theresa explained: "I escaped from my reality every time I did drugs. That's what I was doing, escaping. It helped me escape from life for quite awhile."

Participants' use of alcohol and/or drug use helped them to manage how they felt about their selves in this phase. Because most women were having difficulty "living" with themselves, alcohol and/or drugs provided a means of escaping the selves that they did not like. As Rivka explained: "Addiction is when you are using something to the extent that it's the most important thing. It's the thing that you're living for."

For three participants—Martha, Phoebe, and Fran—who used in isolation, substances helped them to deal with personal problems. For example, Martha explained that she was a solitary drinker: "I didn't go out and drink. I drank at home." Although Martha did work during the week, she had no social life and drank on weekends. After her divorce from an abusive husband, she intentionally isolated herself:

> I didn't have any friends left. Most of them were married couples, and when married couples have a party, they don't usually invite an odd person unless they are inviting an extra man or something, or an extra lady. I just didn't, those five years after my divorce, I didn't do much of anything. I never went to a movie. I did not have television. I read a lot. I had a lot of time to myself. I spent a lot of time with my dogs.

Martha was using alcohol in order to hide her hurt from the breakup of her marriage: "I had to hide in that bottle to get away from all that hurt I was going through. Uh-huh, I had to hide in that to get me through what I was going through."

For Phoebe, whose drug of choice was also alcohol, life was "spinning out of control." She clarified her situation at the time:

> My son was out of control on drugs. My grandfather had died. I had taken care of him until he passed. This was all in the same year, '98. Within three months, I had lost him. A good friend's son hung himself and then my son's best friend was sitting next to him and pulled the trigger of a gun under his chin and killed himself. My whole life was spinning out of control. I took my daughter, left my husband, left my eighteen-year-old and moved out into the woods, shut my business down and proceeded to drink myself to death.

Fran was addicted to the prescription drug Darvocet: her use was also solitary. Having been prescribed the drug by her physician for pain resulting from an automobile accident, she later forged his signature in order to obtain more after he would no longer prescribe them for her:

> The doctor prescribed them at the hospital and after I was released from the hospital, the doctor kept me on them. And it got so I couldn't do without them even after, even if I didn't have no pain, I was after them. And it seemed like when I saw myself getting low, it was like, I got to get 'em, I got to get 'em. It's just like I'm going to every doctor in the county to get them.

Fran did manage to receive the drug from various doctors: "I mean people that didn't know me, you know, like the doctors; they seemed to sympathize with me."

Martha, Phoebe, and Fran were using alcohol and/or drugs for reasons that differed from those of other participants. They were using in order to cope with personal family problems. Fran, even after she no longer had any pain, wanted to continue using because she "felt like I needed them" and "they kept me from hurting."

In this phase, participants found a new way of dealing with themselves and with their problems through use of substances: alcohol and/or drugs offered them other sources of meaning. Whether it was for pleasure, fun, coping with problems, alcohol and/or drugs provided them with a sense of release from problems. Most participants were "inundated"[19] in an alcohol and/or drug world.

Opportunity to use and access to alcohol and/or drugs were significant for twenty-two participants in this phase, as they were now using and identifying with significant others, another reference group that consisted of alcohol and/or drug users as well. There is an indication here that participants had created meanings within a social context of addiction and had established a sense of themselves within this environment. Substances had now become central to their lives. They now had a social relationship with a social object that was providing them with significant meanings in their lives. For some participants, it was the social world of alcohol and/or drug culture that gave them fun and pleasure; social circumstances and significant others in this social world were attractive to them in this phase. For others, it was the fact that use of substances provided them with the means to deal with problems in their lives. Participants sought many things in the alcohol and/or drugs they used that they were unable to find elsewhere. They found relationships, acceptance, relief, fun, and pleasure. Their experiences were now meaningful, gratifying, and self-reinforcing.

The following section provides insights into participants' experiences of immersion into addicted selves and how this phase was working for them. In *The Immersed Drug Self* phase, participants were managing addiction through various means.

The Immersed Drug Self

> The truth was quickly clouded over with the need to drink and to change myself. The thing about hallucinogenic drugs was that because I was an addict, I never wanted to come down. I didn't want to come back to reality. (Kathleen)

As Kathleen stated in the above quote, addiction was central to her life at this time, as it was for all participants. The quotes discussed below demonstrate how women were managing immersed, addicted selves through various means. Participants talked about complete immersion in an alcohol and/or drug world, which included prostitution, selling drugs, and using drugs. The problem of using substances pushed one participant into dealing drugs and two into prostitution.

As participants talked about this phase in their addiction, they made it very clear that this time was "normal" for them. In other words, participants were not in denial. Instead, they were pursuing a life of addiction and living with the consequences. For example, Hannah said: "I really liked to do drugs. It was like I was hiding, I felt like being secretive and trying to hide things." Marie noted that she "didn't have too many consequences, so I kind of really enjoyed drinking." And Robbie's attitude was nonchalant:

> I could mix drinks. I could drink from the beginning to the end and never get drunk or anything. I had a high tolerance and people used to say, "How in the world do you do that and never have a hangover or anything?" And I used to laugh, I'd say, "You've either got it or you don't." It was all a game. Whatever was happening, it happened.

Participants mentioned how harmful this time had been to them and to important others in their lives. They literally did "bury themselves in drugs." They were experiencing encapsulated selves in an encapsulated social world of alcohol and/or drug use in this phase. Many times in our interviews, women stressed that this was the first time they had been given the opportunity to consider past experiences and to look back at immersions in an alcohol and/or drug culture. Even though they may have narrated their stories in Alcoholics Anonymous (AA), Narcotics Anonymous (NA), or with a counselor, the interviews seem useful because they helped participants put their pasts in perspective in a nonjudgmental analysis.

I found the following two characteristics in this phase of participants' lives: (1) social identities were emerging for twenty-two participants with key features such as: constant use, relationships with user reference groups, and settings relevant to women's using, and (2) management actions around addiction were relevant for all participants.

A major descriptor in this phase of participants' lives was the identity of "drug addict" or "alcoholic" that they took on as they explained their feelings toward themselves and their immersion in an alcohol and/or drug culture. But, in this full immersion, they had to learn how to manage addiction as well. Participants all related that a key feature of being an addict was its everyday occurrence. They used constantly during the day and/or during the nighttime. A second common feature among twenty-two of the participants was that their use of alcohol and/or drugs was a collective social occurrence in which they used only with other addicts. These addicts had now become their reference groups. A third social reference point was their use in bars or at parties with other users. A fourth feature was the similarity of these participants' lives to those of other users: many participants related that they had become what they termed, "druggies."

Women's Experiences within an Alcohol and/or Drug Culture

Participants had now procured addictive identities, and for twenty-two participants these identities were integral to how they wanted to see themselves in this phase. For example, looking back at her experiences, Grace signified that her constant use was a key feature in her "druggie" identity: "I'd wake up drinking. I'd go to bed drinking. I'd wake up in the middle of the night drinking, go back to bed, start all over again. I would consider myself an alcoholic and a druggie."

Deb's immersion was predominantly a social occurrence because she often used with others. It was a social time for her and provided her with a social identity as a party drinker:

> When I'd go out drinking, I couldn't just have one or two. I was drinking to the point, I shouldn't say never, I mean occasionally, I could have one or two, but normally, I was drinking until intoxication. And, a lot of times that would mean I'd be up all night partying. I wouldn't even stop at bar time. Which I, I was a bar drinker, you know. When I wasn't drinking, I wasn't as social. It was kind of like, that I needed that to, um, break down those defenses.

Robbie's description of her usage taking place at a bar provides a good example of regular social patterns. She noted her loyalty to her local bar, her social reference point in this phase. These experiences were part of a common pattern in her life:

> The band [at the bar] wasn't there on Sunday and Monday nights, but I was, you know. I felt I was loyal. And that was a pattern for almost

> all my drinking right up until the end. Wherever I moved I found my bar and that was the place I went. I went every single night and I went from the sweetheart at the bar to the bitch on the corner, but it just took me years. I felt like I fit in when I drank and it was the whole "bar" thing. I didn't bar hop too much.

Sandy's experiences exemplify the fourth feature of the addict, that is, her usage and socialization took place with similar significant others. She noted that her use was a normal, everyday occurrence within her family, who were all drug dealers, and with other substance users: "I never had friends. My family was all drug dealers. I never needed to go outside my family. The hard [part] for me is being raised on drugs and alcohol. It's much easier when life ain't going your way to roll up a joint and say to hell with it."

Theresa's drug use was helping her create a new social reality and helping her "feel completely different." She analyzed, very well, how her drug of choice, cocaine, was her "best friend" by explaining how it changed and altered her self-image:

> Drugs overpower your body. They are mind-altering, they change; they completely change your personality while you're on the drug. Sometimes people have long effects and it completely changes them for the rest of their lives. It is your best friend while you are using. It is absolutely your best friend. I mean, you're down and out, depressed, whatever. Do a line, everything's great. I mean, it does. It takes away any type of problem you have. It doesn't matter what it is. You could have lost someone in your life. One line, that'll make you feel better. It puts you in a different mind set. It just like throws you out there and makes you feel completely different.

In this phase, some participants specified that they were using substances in what they termed a subculture of users. They were very clear as they talked about situations in which they used alcohol and/or drugs. For example, Hannah said that she "was in a subculture. I mean I had my using friends, I mean everybody wants to fit in with somebody." Similarly, Tracy stated, "I wasn't really in society. I was in a subculture."

Shirley was unusual in that she became not only a user but a drug seller, as well. She commented on this experience:

> I was a million-dollar drug dealer—first-class flights, limousines, tables full of drugs, penthouse suites, parties that lasted a week, a nanny. I mean drugs were my life. [I knew] everything about drugs. I read books. I educated myself; I threw experimental parties for sessions with Ecstasy. I mean I have done raw crystal acid. I never had a waking moment where I wasn't on something for so many years. Yeah, I was a druggie.

For participants who used in isolation, different factors impinged on their alcohol and/or drug use. Martha's usage of alcohol was to get "some peace and quiet" away from her abusive environment. Phoebe was using alcohol to "drink herself to death." Fran's use of the prescription drug Darvocet was to "keep from hurting."

The women immersed themselves in an alcohol and/or drug culture and a lifestyle that was normal for them. They were in a society of users that provided them with some degree of comfort, and the women saw themselves as similar to their significant others: drug addicts, alcoholics, or "druggies."

A version of symbolic interactionism is labeling theory.[20] Becker focuses on societal reaction to deviant acts (i.e., drug use) in his studies in the sociology of deviance. Becker argues that "[s]ocial groups create deviance by making rules whose infraction constitutes deviance, and by applying those rules to particular people and labeling them as outsiders."[21]

Deviance results from the consequences of the responses of others to a person's act, thus resulting in the labeling of that person.[22] Therefore, deviance results as a consequence of interaction between people in society. Labeling theory clarifies the process of social control.[23] Although labeling theory does not address the initial question of why people choose to break society's rules, it does provide an increased understanding of how individuals might take on negative labels through their deviant acts. And, more importantly, whether an act is considered deviant or not depends on how people react to it, not on the nature of the activity itself.

Becker[24] sees the process of becoming deviant in terms of a series of phases that leads to the individual's deviance becoming a "master status," that "feature of the person that is most important to him or her as well as to others."[25] This puts labeling theory in the camp of symbolic interactionism: a dynamic process of definition and interpretation comprising interaction between those in society who apply the label and a consideration of what consequences such labeling has for the person so labeled. For example, many women interviewed for this study underscored self-labeling as they "took on" the deviant label of "druggies." Even the fact that they mentioned it to me was an indication that they "knew" themselves as addicts, declaring their assertion of social identities while addicted. Conversely, as participants recovered, they talked to me about "recovering" identities, indicating that social identities had again changed. They did not consider themselves in recovery as having social identities as "addicts" any longer.

How Women Managed Their Addictions

Participants shared common features as they were managing addiction. Whether participants were working or going to school at this time, addiction was helping them manage the social and individual discomforts they felt in dealing with themselves and with others. As Nancy stated, she was managing her difficulty by integrating her line of action into joint action with others:

> What the alcohol used to do is alleviate that discomfort from being around other people, it kind of smoothes the way. It allows me to be more verbal, more personable and not be so sensitive to other peo-

> ple's moods. It kind of, it kind of just smoothes the discomfort of just living in the human race.

In this phase of participants' lives, it was notable that, for many women, immersion in alcohol and/or drug lives was an everyday occurrence. As Phoebe commented, alcohol use was a necessary action that helped her manage her day, and she was what she terms a "functioning drunk": "Addiction, for me, was something that I had to do everyday. It's controlling. I felt in my mind that I had to have it every day to get me through my day. I was a functioning drunk. I sewed. I went to work every day. I cut hair on the side when I was working a different job."

For Rivka, a consequence of addiction was that she had to drop out of school because she was having difficulty in managing both school and her drinking: "I was drinking so much that I had to drop out of school. I can't tell you how many glasses, but getting drunk most nights of the week. I was drinking a lot of amaretto, a lot of beer, you know, drinking during the week so I couldn't go to class in the morning."

Hannah managed not only to work a full-time job but also to smoke marijuana at work, planning her life around her addiction:

> Well, I would smoke from the time I got up in the morning to the time that I would go to bed at night. I would smoke at work. I worked in a group home for the mentally retarded, so me and my friend, that I am still friends with, you know, we met there, but we would go down in the basement, where the washroom was, you know, the washer and dryer. We made a pipe out of a paper towel roll, and we'd smoke [marijuana] there. So, yeah, I planned my life around my drug use.

Lynn, too, managed not only to start nursing school but also to use while working in a hospital after she graduated:

> From sixteen to age twenty when I started nursing school, I always dealt drugs and I also got two years of college. It's not that we're not ambitious as alcoholics. We're very ambitious. A lot of times I had three jobs at a time because I always knew I needed enough money to do the drugs. Then when I graduated from nursing school I started shooting up at work [with morphine and Demerol]. I had no using friends when I was doing drugs at the hospital. I did this all by myself. I would go to the bathroom, do my drugs, go back and work. Everybody thought I was such a great worker because I was always working. Your whole life is the drugs. Nothing else matters.

Kathleen also incorporated alcohol into her daily life and managed to stay in school: "I used on a daily basis, I mean there might have been an occasional day that I didn't drink, but it was far and few between. I drank a lot and went to nursing school and graduated with an associate degree in nursing." What seems unusual for participants in this phase was that seven were using alcohol and/or drugs while working and three were in school. Another participant (Shirley) was both a dealer and a user: her job was selling drugs. Another participant, Esther, left her job in order to manufacture her drug of choice, Ecstasy.

Participants by this point had procured addictive identities, as well as identities that "fitted" with how they wanted to see themselves as individuals. Personal, social, and situated identities corresponded with significant others within the addict world. How people locate themselves and one another in social life is an important aspect within the symbolic interactionist paradigm; it provides integration and continuity within society.

In this section, I have highlighted how twenty-two participants saw themselves as part of an alcohol and/or drug culture as they became totally immersed into a community of other users. For three participants, substance use provided them with the means to deal with specific problems in their lives. But alcohol and/or drugs now began to turn against them, and they perceived that substances were no longer working for them. They became filled with self-loathing and disgusted with themselves as they started to see how their actions were affecting their lives in a negative way.

The Disgusted Self

> I was thinking suicide. I became thoroughly disgusted with myself. I was so self-loathing. (Nancy)

Participants, immersed in an alcohol and/or drug culture with other users, had become "situated"[26] within a social milieu that provided them with individual and social meanings. As immersion in addiction progressed for these women, they procured identities that fitted with how they saw themselves as individuals. Finally, participants came to a phase in which they began to realize that the alcohol and/or drugs they were using either had run their course or were no longer working as they formerly had. As Nancy noted in the above quote, the women began to scrutinize addicted selves in different ways.

In *The Disgusted Self* phase of addictive careers, participants began to change how they felt about themselves. Slowly they had to deal with the effects of alcohol and/or drug use and how it had affected them over the months or years they had been using. My purpose in this section, then, is to explore how participants' individual selves became self-loathing and how alcohol and/or drug use began to "turn on them." The substances they had been using in addiction were no longer making them feel good, either physically or socially.

Two characteristics predominated participants' narratives in this phase: (1) feelings of self-disgust began to emerge, and (2) coercion was a salient factor for four participants in this phase that led to feelings of self-disgust as they were forced into recovery. Participants discussed various feelings that began to emerge, slowly shifting feelings about themselves. As participants looked back at this time in their lives, they revealed concerns they had about themselves in this phase.

In *The Disgusted Self* phase, negative impacts of alcohol and/or drugs were emerging in the lives of participants, often reported in terms like "I was no longer in love [with the alcohol]," "I had self-hate," "I felt depressed," "I felt terrible," "I felt worthless," "I started thinking I had a problem," and "I became so sick." Feelings of self-disgust and worthlessness were common among many participants. Others mentioned how depressed and "terrible" they felt toward the end of their addicted phases. Ironically, the same nineteen participants who earlier had talked about their addicted selves as people who used alcohol and/or drugs in order to alleviate negative feelings about themselves within a negative social environment were now experiencing a growing sense of self-disgust in this phase.

Women's Sense of Self-Disgust

Participants' feelings of disgust toward themselves were a response to the failure of particular lines of action in this phase—that is, addiction was no longer working for them as it once had. It seemed as though their alcohol and/or drug use had now come full circle: their initial reason for using was to help them with such feelings of worthlessness and depression. Now alcohol and/or drugs had turned against them and they had to consider what they would have to do to have an alcohol and/or drug-free life and what would replace this "best friend" that no longer worked for them. In a sense, these participants were back to how they initially felt about themselves.

Participants' sense of selves was changing in this phase. The majority of them referred to the significance of individual selves and social identities, not explicitly, but in a subtle fashion. The negative impacts that their lives as addicts had upon their sense of selves were reported in the form of a great unhappiness with the sort of individuals they had become. This was expressed in a variety of ways. For instance, Kathleen comments on her feelings of self-loathing by stating that she was at the "point of putting a gun" to her head as she explained: "I was just, ah, couldn't stand being inside of me and I didn't see any solutions."

As Lynn considered quitting, her feelings were of self-hate, something that she has trouble with in her life. Obviously, the self-hate she experienced in addiction seemed to parallel the self-hate she had experienced prior to her usage: "I'm still trying to figure out why I hate myself. However, I'm getting better."

Health concerns plagued some participants. Although many had been ill for some time, they finally came to a point in their lives when they became, as many of the women said, "sick and tired of being sick and tired" with themselves for using. For example, Hannah provided a good overview:

> Yeah, I was starting to taper off. I went through this binge of pills. Like I said, I always smoked marijuana. That was like the core element to everything, but I went through this period of [taking] pills, and I would even like crush them up and snort them like that and, you know, I would get nose bleeds and I was starting to vomit all the time, and I wasn't eating and, um, I think that was sort of like the be-

> ginning of the end. You know, I was taking more and more [pills] and I was just so sick and tired all the time. Just sick and tired and so I guess the things inside of me started to shift and started to change.

Hannah became suicidal as a consequence of her bad health: "I wanted to die. There was this repetitive thought in my mind, 'You are not going to wake up, you are going to die.' So it was like the fear of dying and not wanting to die, but yet wanting to die. It just, it gets so twisted up. Everything gets so tangled or twisted up." She provided a succinct comment on the control aspect of drugs and how she experienced it. Although substances had been "functional" for her in addiction, she came to see drugs as "dysfunctional" in that they were no longer "fun" and no longer had a purpose for her: "When it got to the point where they [the drugs] control you, you don't control them, and it totally controls your life, that you become dysfunctional, you don't have any purpose, you don't have anything else to give, then they're not fun anymore." There was a parallel in this phase of participants' lives. Most participants had turned to alcohol and/or drugs because of a lack of a sense of control in early experimental and addicted phases. Conversely, as they were beginning to leave addiction, they were also beginning to lack a sense of control in their use of substances. I argue that in this phase, while alcohol and/or drugs were still physically addictive to participants, these women still saw themselves very much as authors of their own behaviors, able and responsible for developing new lines of action as they moved toward recovery.

Linda's comments mirrored Hannah's as she explained how her thinking about what she was doing to herself began to change:

> I guess I was getting sick. I mean, I was having really bad hangovers. I was working and I can remember what I was doing, I was waiting tables, but I just needed to stop being sick all the time. You know, I mean, I just felt yucky and I knew I wasn't going to get anywhere if I didn't straighten up. I just didn't feel like drinking anymore. I think, I think it was just time for me to stop. I think I was on my way up from the pits of despair in terms of being a drunk all the time. I really felt bad sometimes—physically rotten when I was coming off a three-day drunk, whatever it was, but, yuck, you know, I don't want to do this to myself anymore.

Finally, Mary related how she was becoming "tired" of this self that was constantly using drugs and how she wanted something else for herself: "I was, you know, I wanted to go back to being without drugs in my system. I wanted that for myself, you know, as a long-term goal."

Carol's life as an addict was becoming impossible because she was constantly sick from alcohol use. She was raising two daughters as a single mother and was starting to realize that her use of alcohol was becoming "my first thought in the morning before I thought of feeding my kid a bowl of cereal." She talked about how she realized that she had to do something about this:

> I mean I was throwing up blood. I was very sick, I could not eat. All's I could do was drink beer and, um, it was making me physically sick. I was puking blood. I wouldn't eat for three or four days. I was just laying there drunk in a pile of beer cans mainly every day. I mean, it was always my first thought in the morning, you know, so I knew what I had to do.

Rhonda stated directly that her drug of choice, alcohol, had "stopped working," making her feel miserable and not fulfilling its previous function: "It wasn't doing anything for me anymore, making me feel like, totally, miserable.

In *The Disgusted Self* phase, although many participants had been ill for a period of time, there came the time when they could no longer continue to feel this way. Something had shifted in their feelings about themselves, along with their feelings about substances that had "stopped working," as Rhonda attests. The key to a successful exit from alcohol and/or drug use was to stop because they no longer wanted to be users, in short, to do it because they wanted to change their selves.

Ebaugh[27] in her study of role-exit addresses an important question: the "whys" and "hows" of becoming an "ex." Ebaugh's work on role-exit considered twelve ex-alcoholics (six females and six males) out of a total of 185 individuals who were exiting other roles. She argues that this potential for new lines of action is part of a role-exit that leads to cuing behavior indicating discontent with one's role. The cues for participants in this study were similar in that there were those signs, conscious or unconscious, that showed that they were feeling dissatisfied in their current roles. For example, Shirley's drinking was "killing" her which was a cue that something had to change in her life as she said, "And it just got to the point that I knew I had to do something about it because I felt like I was killing myself, I mean, I drank all day long."

Several researchers[28] argue that rock-bottom episodes are a common occurrence in former addicts' lives. Participants interviewed in this study did not mention rock-bottom episodes per se, but feelings of hitting a bottom in terms of pain and suffering related to how they felt about themselves. Although the "bottom" differs among participants, it is always an emotional low point for them. Women highlight how these feelings toward their selves were helping them to see that if they did not change, they might have nervous breakdowns, go "crazy," die, or commit suicide. For example, Pat stated that she was about to be overcome by the effects of alcohol:

> I think I was kind of having a nervous breakdown and what it was, I wasn't going to drink but I didn't have anything in its place and so it was like I wanted to drink, but I wasn't going to drink and I wasn't going to, you know, and I just thought I was going to die. I just thought I was going to explode, you know, and I really had this feeling of suicide that I just wasn't going to commit suicide, so I thought it was just going to happen, that it was going to just overcome me.

This was the moment when she finally decided that she needed help with addiction:

> I went [to AA], and it was just like an hour of peace where my head wasn't just rambling and rolling and, you know, driving me crazy, and it relieved that, that feeling of wanting to drink. And I don't think I heard much of anything except for just this calm, you know. I don't remember what I heard, I remember people being happy, and I remember wanting to go back, but, then, I went home and analyzed it, and thought, well, yeah, I would go again.

Tracy related how her life was "falling apart" and her thoughts were of suicide: "And I got sick and tired of being sick and tired. I got tired of living [this way]." Phoebe also described her experience in similar terms: "I used to think I was an endless pit."

A number of these women referred to two factors in this phase: (1) how alcohol and/or drug usage was "killing" them, or (2) how they thought about attempting suicide. I argue that these two factors were related: either way, participants' actions were taking them to negative ends. Perhaps they were becoming disgusted with addictive selves because they saw themselves engaging in a self-annihilation that was unacceptable to them.

Participants were recognizing that something was wrong in their selves and they needed to pay attention to such feelings of self-disgust. They were beginning to realize that something was skewed in their sense of selves and that they needed to counter negative self-feelings in this phase.

Elements of Coercion in Some Women's Lives

Not all participants began feeling self-disgust in this phase: four were coerced into stopping their alcohol and/or drug use. But three of these participants reiterated a differing sense of selves as they looked back and talked about themselves when they were forced to quit. The first participant, Fran, had forged a prescription for Darvocet and was put on probation. As she says, "Well, they didn't want to send me to prison just for being on drugs. It had to be more serious." Fran was ordered by the judge to attend Health Recovery Services (HRS) at this time. Only after this did Fran realize that if she had continued, she would "be dead." She found quitting very difficult: "The hardest was leaving them alone [the Darvocet]. Leaving them alone, cause if I knew that I took them, my probation officer got them in my urine, found them in my urine, I was done with. I know better than to mess with her."

Sandy was addicted to marijuana and alcohol from age five to age twenty-nine within a family of users and dealers. At age twenty-nine she was arrested for domestic violence against a husband who was abusive to her as well. As she stated:

> It was at my husband, I had had one big fit and was throwin' some dishes around and he called the cops on me and they arrested me for—they tried to get me for domestic violence. But they dropped it

> to a misdemeanor if I agreed to do the HRS thing. They did that—that all I had to do was see a drug counselor.

Because she was pregnant at the time, the court insisted that she be subject to urine testing. Thus, she had no choice "but to quit." But because she was coerced into doing so, she thought: "They were trying to kill me. I didn't understand why I could not smoke pot. It took me a few months. I was rebellious. I still believed that there was nothing wrong with smoking marijuana. Okay, I can drink and take pills, but there wasn't nothing wrong with marijuana." Then, Sandy began to realize that the courts might take the baby away when it was born; this cemented her abstinence and began her process of recovery.

Rhonda talked about being "forced" into quitting her alcohol use. She received a felony DUI (driving under the influence) conviction, and the court mandated her into a rehabilitation center: "I went into rehab pretty well intoxicated and they made the decision for me. I realized that I was heading either to prison, or death was my next option and I didn't feel like going to either one of them."

Esther was eventually sent to a woman's prison in the state for manufacturing Ecstasy in an isolated farmhouse that she had rented. During our interview time together, she was still on probation and will be for five years. Esther did not believe that her addiction was a physical one, but that she was "definitely mentally addicted because I became obsessed by it." She continued to relate her feelings about Ecstasy:

> After I was arrested was, one part of me, I was so upset with the choices that I had made that put me in this place [prison] and really disappointed with myself because I felt like I had more to offer than being labeled a number or being in the [prison] system and that type of thing. But I really had a very large sadness in me for the Ecstasy and the way that it is viewed by a lot of, I don't know whether you would say, law enforcement or this DARE America and that type of thing. Because I do, and there, there is goodness in it if taken responsibly and perhaps if you can say in a controlled environment, I could see where it would be so beneficial in certain cases.

Esther highlighted that she would "possibly get off paper in two and one-half years. So three years after that, I'll be able to get it [her felony] expunged."

One way or another, participants talked about how dysfunctional alcohol and/or drugs had become for them in this phase. Twenty-four women highlighted the fact that substances no longer had a purpose for them. Something had shifted in participants' feelings toward themselves, along with how they were now constructing different meanings toward alcohol and/or drugs. I argue that most participants had become disenchanted with participation in an alcohol and/or drug culture. Their selves had become corrupted, and addicted lifestyles allowed them no room for self-respect. The cost of continuing alcohol and/or drug use had become too great to continue, they no longer wished to be part of the addicted life; therefore, they began to evaluate alternative lifestyles within recovery.

This section has highlighted how participants finally had begun to consider stopping their use of alcohol and/or drugs and some of the varying feelings they were having about themselves that compelled them to begin to do so. Even though there were common characteristics among most of these women in *The Disgusted Self* phase, perhaps Robbie stated it most clearly when she evaluated how her drug of choice "gave up" on her and how she had a glimpse of an alternative self:

> It was no longer my dream, my lover. I was no longer in love (with the alcohol). It no longer was the success story . . . [I had] that little tiny glimpse that it didn't have to be the way it had begun to be, because as gradual as my recovery has been, my drinking was that gradual down into the bottom. But that little glimpse of that being different, I think that's what got it. And every time I was able to stay sober, and something worked, that I worked through, that I managed to make it [into her recovery].

Summary

In this chapter, I have explored participants' insights into their addicted selves, ranging from the time when their use of alcohol and/or drugs had been a pleasurable time, through their immersion in addictive careers, and, finally, their ending addiction with disgusted feelings about addictive selves. The women's narratives clearly showed how they traveled from addiction into the beginning of their recovery, whereby they now had to learn how to manage recovering selves. They had been able to "beat the dragon of their addiction"[29] as they left addictive behaviors behind and began journeys to recovery.

These participants composed alternate selves incompatible with excessive alcohol and/or drug use through new avenues and new meanings.[30] The following chapter provides an exploration of recovering selves for participants as they become aware of how individual and social selves are changing, along with how they begin to strategize in recovery processes, coupled with how they continue with stable selves.

Notes

1. T. Shibutani, *Social Processes: An Introduction to Sociology* (Berkeley, CA: University of California, 1986), 164.
2. T. Shibutani, *Society and Personality: An Interactionist Approach to Social Psychology* (Englewood Cliffs, NJ: Prentice Hall, 1961), 164.
3. C. Terry, *The Fellas: Overcoming Prison and Addiction* (Belmont, CA: Wadsworth/Thomson Learning, 2003), 13.
4. Shibutani, *Society and Personality*, 164.
5. Shibutani, *Society and Personality*, 164.
6. E. Goode, *Drugs in American Society,* fifth ed. (Boston: McGraw-Hill, 1999),

226.

7. J. Bynum and W. Thompson, *Juvenile Delinquency: A Sociological Approach,* 6th ed. (Boston: Allyn and Bacon, 2005).

8. D. Brownfield, "Adolescent Male Status and Delinquent Behavior," *Sociological Spectrum* 10 (April–June 1990): 227–48; D. Kandel, "On Processes of Peer Influence in Adolescent Drug Use: A Developmental Perspective," *Advances in Alcohol and Substance Use* 4 (Spring-Summer 1985): 139–63; Z. T. McGee, "Social Class Differences in Parental and Peer Influence on Adolescent Drug Use," *Deviant Behavior* 13 (October–December 1992): 349–72.

9. Substance Abuse and Mental Health Services Administration (SAMHSA), *Results from the 2003 National Survey on Drug Use and Health* (Washington, DC: Department of Health and Human Services, 2004).

10. M. Adrian, C. Lundy, and M. Eliany, eds., *Canadian Women and Substance Use: Overview and Policy Implications* (Toronto, Ontario: Addiction Research Foundation, 1996).

11. SAMHSA, *Results from the 2003 National Survey on Drug Use and Health.*

12. J. F. Donnermeyer, "The Use of Alcohol, Marijuana, and Hard Drugs by Rural Adolescents: A Review of Recent Research," *Drugs and Society* 50 (1992): 31–77.

13. SAMHSA, *Results from the 2003 National Survey on Drug Use and Health.*

14. S. Peele, *The Diseasing of America: Addiction Treatment out of Control* (Lexington, MA: Lexington Books, 1989).

15. M. Rosenbaum, *Women on Heroin* (New Brunswick, NJ: Rutgers University Press, 1981), 35.

16. S. Brown, *Treating the Alcoholic: A Developmental Model of Recovery* (New York: John Wiley and Sons, 1985), 153.

17. Rosenbaum, *Women on Heroin,* 48.

18. R. Broadhead, *Inundation of Family Life: The Impact of Professional Socialization on the Families of Medical Students* (Los Angeles: University of California Press, 1978).

19. Rosenbaum, *Women on Heroin*, 48.

20. H. Becker, *Outsiders* (New York: Free Press), 1963.

21. Becker, *Outsiders.*

22. Becker, *Outsiders.*

23. N. Heitzeg, *Deviance: Rulemakers and Rulebreakers* (Minneapolis, MN: West, 1996).

24. Becker, *Outsiders*, 33.

25. R. Regoli and J. Hewitt, *Delinquency in Society,* fourth ed. (Boston: McGraw-Hill, 2000), 148.

26. J. Hewitt, *Self and Society: A Symbolic Interactionist Social Psychology*, ninth ed. (Boston: Allyn and Bacon, 2003), 141.

27. H. R. F. Ebaugh, *Becoming an Ex: The Process of Role-Exit* (Chicago: University of Chicago Press, 1988).

28. P. Biernacki, *Pathways from Heroin Addiction: Recovery without Treatment* (Philadelphia: Temple University Press, 1986); N. Denzin, *The Recovering Alcoholic* (Newbury Park, CA: Sage, 1987b); S. Maruna, *Making Good: How Ex-Convicts Reform and Rebuild Their Lives* (Washington, DC: American Psychological Association, 2001); J. McIntosh and N. McKeganey, *Beating the Dragon: The Recovery from Dependent Drug Use* (Harlow, England: Prentice Hall, 2002).

29. McIntosh and McKeganey, *Beating the Dragon,* 41.

30. H. Becker, "Becoming a Marijuana User," *American Journal of Sociology* 59 (1953): 235–42; Biernacki, *Pathways from Heroin Addiction.*

Chapter 4

The Recovering Self

Introduction

> If a stable form of a new behavior toward . . . [an] object is to emerge, a transformation of meanings must occur, in which the person develops a new conception of the nature of the object.[1]

In the preceding discussion, I have shown how participants became involved in addictive environments through addicted selves. Through this involvement, the women moved from a sense of pleasure to full immersion in lifestyles of alcohol and/or drug use. Whether this transition was short or long, addiction eventually filled them with a sense of self-disgust.

As Becker[2] notes, the argument for change was mirrored in participants' experiences as they discussed how they reevaluated alcohol and/or drug use as the meanings they had assigned to substances began to change and as they participated in ongoing evaluations of themselves while moving into recovery processes. Understanding the meanings of substances (the social object) for participants as they related alcohol and/or drug use to themselves (now as nonusers) allowed me to tap into the social meanings of recovery for these women.

The following discussion highlights women's processes of moving away from self-disgust and toward reconstituting a sense of their selves as they left addiction behind and began to enter recovery processes. It is important to recognize in this study that I am not suggesting that participants completely recover—there is no such thing, as my participants made plain to me. There are varying levels of intervention on both a personal and institutional level as women struggle to abstain. But it forever affects the way they go about their lives, and it never completely heals.[3] Shirley clarified this idea as she talked about her recovery process: "It's a never-ending journey."

What was of interest in this phase of participants' lives was the answer to the question that I posed during our interviews: "Do you think you gained a new sense of self or a new identity in your recovery process?" This question elicited involved and thoughtful answers from these women. In their lengthy reflections, the women did not talk about proceeding in a linear progression from being addicts to becoming nonaddicts, but about halting struggles.

As the meanings assigned to alcohol and/or drugs of choice changed, participants' meanings toward themselves also underwent changes. They came to realize that they had to relinquish their addictions, to become nonaddicts, and to work actively to establish new individual selves and social identities. By engaging with nonaddicts, these women eventually shaped their selves into new identities as recovered addicts.

This chapter is divided into three sections: (1) *The Aware Self*, which includes experiences of how women generated new individual selves and new social identities in recovery; (2) *The Strategic Self*, which consists of the actions the women performed in order to enter and stay in recovery; and (3) *The Stable Self*, which takes account of the women's ongoing abstinent lives. I suggest that key to achieving and maintaining a substance-free status was the participants' abilities to take on new identities and roles as nonaddicts by transforming the central relationships through which they structured new selves and new social identities.

Overcoming addiction is a gradual process, one distinguished by early and later phases.[4] Common, yet unique challenges characterize each phase. Although the women related that their experiences of recovery were journeys of change, they also went though periods of relapse and other challenges to their ongoing abstinence.

The purpose of the following section, *The Aware Self*, is to understand how participants became aware of how their individual and social selves were changing as they began to process alternative, nonaddicted selves. Many participants had used alcohol and/or drugs with others; they had been part of a community of users. Their "situated identities"[5] had provided them with the framework whereby they acted as addicts; they had been immersed or engrossed in addictive identities for some time. Situated identities, however, are always linked to social and personal identities.[6] As participants became aware of their need to change, they understood that they needed to acquire new social selves/identities within new social locations. This involved engaging with significant others in different social environments. It involved making sustained connections and interactions with nonusing others in order to recover from addiction. Identification with a community of nonusers allowed participants opportunities to experience themselves as nonaddicts. Their social identities "by definition acknowledges the importance of other members of the community with which the person identifies and views their influence as valuable."[7] Their social identities changed to those of nonaddicts in communities of nonusers.

Addiction had been meaningful only insofar as it had been functional for them. Now, in participants' aware phases, use of alcohol and/or drugs was no longer meaningful; therefore, they needed to find other self-images that were congruent with their need to see themselves as nonaddicts. Participants needed to change what they had been doing (their addiction) because it was no longer working for them.

In *The Aware Self* phase of addiction, many participants continued to have health problems and were often sick from use of substances. Many stated that it was just "time to quit" or that "it was just time." Other women commented that it was their "last chance to recover and to live." In *The Aware Self* phase, participants reevaluated alcohol and/or drug use and the consequences/effects it had for their personal and emotional lives, as well as for their health.

The second section, *The Strategic Self*, provides an overview of how participants processed and practiced nonaddicted selves and identities. The final section, *The Stable Self*, highlights the processes of maintaining, consolidating, and integrating new selves and identities into new nonaddictive lives.

The Aware Self

> My inner self changed. I am more aware of what's going on. I can pick up on little things more. I prayed every day to stay sober. (Martha)

As Martha's quote suggests, participants found some important elements in *The Aware Self* phase. Participants related that they were beginning not only to see a different world for themselves but also to feel "different" from previous selves. The following discussion illustrates how participants made initial decisions to end addiction, a process by which they redefined their alcohol and/or drug-using experiences. This section begins to answer the question: "How are participants processing changes as they become aware that they need to change themselves?"

Previously (in *The Addicted Self* phase), participants had health concerns, suicidal tendencies, and general feelings of self-hate for addicted selves. In *The Aware Self* phase, participants became cognizant of their need to change their lives in order to leave addiction behind and to enter recovery. Two characteristics emerged in this phase of participants' lives: (1) All participants became aware of shifting self-images, and (2) all but three participants became aware of their need gradually to disconnect from former using friends and/or partners with whom they had used.

Participants talked about shifts in their self-images as they became aware that their lives needed to change. They were changing because the previous patterns on which their lives had been constructed were becoming increasingly unworkable.[8] In order to activate such changes, participants "must fashion new perspectives and social world involvements wherein the addict identity is excluded or dramatically depreciated."[9]

Whether it was through self-disgust or coercion into recovery by the courts, participants shifted in how they saw and felt about themselves. They became detached from the addictive lifestyle. I argue that the participants' experiences of using alcohol and/or drugs were being transformed and that these experiences contained the "seeds of cessation"[10] as many of the originally sought-after pleasures began to diminish or disappear. In other words, the original euphoria slowly became dysphoria for participants, and the women were feeling unwell and unhappy with a diminished sense of well being.

Participants became aware that they could begin to enter recovery. As will be seen in this chapter, what began as a side bet[11]—for example, aiming to recover, but relapsing nevertheless—would eventually become a full-blown commitment to abstinence. Using Becker's[12] notion of commitment as investment, we can understand the importance of struggling to recover in participants' lives.

It was obvious in this phase that participants wanted to be different persons. This desire cemented the view that social identities were changing within new social contexts that did not include alcohol and/or drugs. No matter how they described new selves, this process of restructuring selves and identities seemed to be a necessary one as women entered recovery.

Twenty-two participants talked about intentionally leaving former using friends as they became aware that they could not enter recovery unless they did so. The remaining three, who used in isolation, also discussed becoming involved in their communities again. Many participants talked about how difficult it was to leave using friends behind and about how they no longer could socialize with them in any capacity. In *The Recovering Self* phase, participants must establish affective bonds with members of a group that offer a solution to their quests for meaning[13] and sever ties with those who might challenge new orientations as they worked toward recovery.

Participants had to establish or reestablish meaningful relationships with individuals whose lives were organized around sobriety.[14] Such relationships helped addicts forge new or restructured selves and identities crucial to recovery. Participants were aware that if they continued to associate with alcohol and/or drug-using friends, they would be tempted to use again. All participants realized the importance of becoming involved in sober lives in order to stay abstinent.

In this first phase of the recovery process, the women highlighted how feelings about themselves changed as they resolved to leave addicted selves behind. Explanations of these new self-images incorporated descriptions of "a new identity," "a restructured identity," "a new stabilizing self," "a spiritual experience," "a reincarnation," and a "transforming process."

Eighteen participants avoided contact with all other users, not only intimates. Avoidance of alcohol and/or drug-using networks was a prerequisite for addicts to dissociate themselves entirely from using friends and from the world of alcohol and/or drugs.[15] As participants illustrated, such former environments contained potential hazards to recovery. Their solutions were to remove themselves from such risks by putting distance, both social and physical, between themselves and former alcohol and/or drug-using companions.

Women's Sense of Shifting Self-Images

The essence of the symbolic interactionist concept of self lies in the idea that individuals can be objects to themselves; it is a fundamental fact of our human existence.[16] As participants talked about a changing sense of self, they were referring back to themselves. Because the self is a social object, it constantly changes as it is defined and redefined in social interactions. It is a process rather than a stable entity.[17]

So the ways in which participants viewed themselves and defined themselves in the following quotes depended on changing social interactions. Identities were the names women called themselves, and usually the name they announced to others that told them who they were.[18] Identities are part of what is meant by self; the two are interconnected. Self is the object toward which one acts; identity is the naming of the self. As some participants told me, both their selves and their identities as addicts changed. It can be argued that this is impression management directed at oneself.[19] As Hewitt explains, "[M]uch of the conversation in which we construct and reconstruct [our biographies] occurs within ourselves and not in interaction with others."[20]

For example, when I asked Theresa about a changing self, she commented that it was only by becoming a different person and leaving her addiction that she was able to generate a new self and a new identity. She emphasized the fact that she became a "different" person as she processed recovery:

> Yes, I'm a different person. I think I'm more aware of what's out there. When you're addicted, I think it's almost blinding. It's like a bright light shining into your face [and] you can't see around it. I do believe you become a different person. You live in denial [when using].

Kathleen talked about how she was no longer what she termed, "this tough cookie," the image she projected when she was using. And even though she could not remember who she "really" was back then, a friend qualified for her that she was not always so "tough," but also was a "caring" person. She stated: "I think that the core of who I was has always been there. It's just that it's been so clouded over and confused during the using years." Kathleen's social identity had changed in the context of her addiction, whereas her individual self had stayed the same. In other words, what she signified as her "core" self had always been present but had been hidden during her using years.

For Nancy, her "original" self was also present, but it had been damaged during her addiction. However, she did highlight the transformation of this "original" self into a "caring" self and described this transformed self more positively:

> I don't think it's a new me. I think it's the original me, the original me before all the damage was done is allowed to come back to life. I believe there is a transformation—from self-loathing to caring. But that's the transformation, because everything I do now is an action that I care about myself where everything I did before was an action that I didn't. Which enables me to make a new identity for myself, a positive one. I was a totally different person [in recovery]. Really everything changed, just a whole, you know, I was reincarnated. That's how it feels, you know, so yeah. It was a spiritual experience. I was feeling a lot of things.

Nancy highlighted how her entry into recovery enabled her to begin to forgive her addicted self for the damage done to herself and to important others in her life. She expanded on these thoughts:

> Recovery is learning to forgive yourself for the damage that you've done through your disease because you damage yourself and other people. So you have to learn to forgive yourself so that you don't want to hurt yourself anymore. That's a real crucial thing. We cannot love each other until we love ourselves, so it's, it's that, it's forgiving yourself, it's learning self-esteem again, to take care of yourself, to value yourself, um, a lot of hope, um, the joy of getting your faculties back, both physical and mental.

Rivka's identity in her addictive career had been suppressed: "I was like somebody different and I was sort of back to myself. So I think during that time [her addiction] it's like that part of me was just suppressed somewhat. My values and those sorts of things were just sort of suppressed."

Mary also talked about how her use of controlled substances suppressed problems for her or "put a blanket over them." For Mary, putting a blanket over problems meant also putting a blanket over her "self," leaving her feeling disconnected. Thus, a feeling of a "disconnected self"[21] developed, a false self that addicts develop in order to separate themselves from feelings, authenticity, and an acceptance of self. As Mary blanketed her "self," she was describing her alienation or separateness from society and others. Ultimately, this blanketed self helped her to abandon herself. It also masked underlying interactional processes embedded in the life of the addict.[22] Thus, deep problematics within the self are anaesthetized through use of alcohol and/or drugs, trapping addicts within a vicious cycle of addiction.[23] Mary reiterated that it was only in recovery that she found her "self," along with her identity:

> I feel I have an identity when I'm in recovery. It's like, it snaps back into me. When I was an addict, I was working at just totally ridding myself of that, you know, of having any identity. I didn't want to know who I was. I didn't want to know what I was feeling, or anything.

Even though Hannah expressed difficulty in answering the question about "self" and a possible new identity, her explanation of her awareness of her past self and of her self change was extensive. For Hannah, her "real" self had always been there, she just had to find it again. In her introspection, she highlighted how she found herself again in recovery:

> I think for the most part, you get a different identity because, you know, going through that, I think it does change you. I definitely think I'm a different person now since I've gone into recovery and I am different. I think my eyes are open more. I'm more aware of what is out there. You learn a lot, I mean you learn to love yourself. It's kind of difficult to describe because it's like finding myself again,

> recognizing that old person. That it was—she was always there. I think, yeah, finding myself. That person that I was always intended to be and now I feel like I have the opportunities to become that person that I've always wanted to be. It's hard to explain.

The recovery process is one of construction and reconstruction of one's identity and resultant view of the world.[24] A new developmental structure, one based on a new identity, is being formed. People in recovery are experiencing a new structure of self-knowledge. Much of the addicts' interpretations of selves and the world no longer fit;[25] therefore, both must be reconstructed. Addicts have to begin to interpret themselves differently along with significant others in their lives. "Restructured" was the descriptive term that Robbie attached to her identity as she related how she had changed her sense of self as she moved into recovery. This restructuring involved a sense of her "owning" her past:

> Q: Would you say that you got a new identity in your recovery?
> Robbie: Restructured, I guess, restructured.
> Q: Okay, in what sense?
> Robbie: Well, it took a long time before I connected with the past, before I could own the past. It was like there and I could not believe that I had done any of that stuff and then this new life. It took a long time before I could say, oh yeah, I did that. It was a long time. And I am grateful that it all worked that way for me.

For Marie, recovery was a self change that provided her with the means to find out who she really was:

> For sure, there's a self change, but when I got into recovery, I didn't know who I was. I think that actually at the beginning of recovery you start discovering yourself, it's almost like finding [out] who you really are. And actually, kind of there we say, whenever you started drinking, you left off at that part of your life at that age.

Shirley also stressed a similar point as she stated that her change, too, was finding out who she truly was in recovery. She reiterated that in her addictive career the objective had been to cover up her "real" identity. In recovery, her identity was "unveiled": "No, I think you find out who you really are. You find out who you really *are,* you unveil your own identity that's been there all the time, but we take on new identities when we drank [participant's emphasis]."

Susan, too, commented in a thoughtful way that "[i]t's the discovery of yourself [in recovery]." Further, she stressed the view that "[i]f you don't set your brain to it, it's not going to happen." Many participants stressed how different they were in recovery from the persons they had been in addictive careers. For example, Deb emphasized, "I'm different now. I was a lot different from that person who was drinking."

Phoebe talked about how, in her self change, she began to like herself more. As she states:

> My identity changed, I like myself today, I'm not a bad person. I have a whole new outlook on life. I'm just a nicer person. Your attitude changes, I just gained a whole new respect for myself. I have more self-esteem. I can explain myself. Now people know who I am because [then] I hid behind the alcohol. I could explain my ideas [in recovery] and so my identity did change. I got to know me.

Part of her identity change in recovery enabled her not only to see herself differently but also to gain insight into the lives of people around her: "The insight, you have an insight a little bit in life maybe. Yes, and I got to know and understand the emotions and feelings of the people around me."

Participants mentioned many times that they finally realized that alcohol and/or drug use was affecting important others in their lives: families, children, and partners. Their primary decisions to enter recovery were motivated by how they initially felt about themselves. They became concerned about significant others after they had decided to do something about how they assessed themselves. It was after they entered recovery that they started to realize that important others in their lives had been affected.

As they developed and changed, the women experienced improvements in relations with families, children, and partners. For example, Ann improved her relationships with her children, her husband, and her mother and father:

> I got to do things with my kids. I got back with my husband and we tried to work things out. Actually we're getting along just fine. I get out and walk. I play games with other people. I like to read books, especially mystery books. I actually turned, you know, turned the world around for me anyway. My family actually started talking to me again cause I quit. I feel like I'm part of the family now.

For Rhonda, changing herself was motivated by her realization that her children were suffering because of her actions. Part of her recovery was to stop disappointing them:

> All the broken promises I gave my girls, my daughters. "I'll quit, I'll quit." All the trouble, like I said, one of them is studying to be a police officer. She's auxiliary right now and it doesn't look good when her mother is being arrested. I was tired of disappointing everybody. I wanted to, I wanted a new fresh life.

As addicts recover, they must learn to be authentic in recovery.[26] Not only must a person accept conventional society in order to maintain recovery, but society must accept that person, as well.[27] For example, during one interview, one woman showed me her "before" picture, a photo of who she was before she became addicted. Then she proceeded to tell me how she is now "like that" once again. Another participant gave me her fifth-year medallion from her Alcoholics Anonymous (AA) program. She said that she valued my research and thought I would like to have it as a memento (I did). But she also, I think, wanted me to trust her as she told me her story and to believe that she was honest about recovery and that it was strong. Maruna calls these "authenticity tests."[28] I argue that addicts use these tests to reduce skepticism among others about their claims about recovery.

Participants talked about how they had disappointed families, partners, and children through their addictive careers. For example, Tracy explained how it took time to regain their trust: "It's very hard for an addict to, ah, not understand why your families are not jumping at the new found recovery you have, you know. Ah, over the years we scam them, we con them, over and over again and it takes a long time for them to trust again." Other participants noted changing relationships as recovery progressed. For example, Hannah talked about how her relationship with her mother had improved: "The relationship with my mum has started to heal in the last couple of years. Our relationship is starting to mend."

Change in the shape of recovery from alcohol and/or drug use is not something visible or objective in the sense it can be proven. It is a construct that is negotiated through interaction between an individual and significant others in a process of "looking-glass rehabilitation."[29] Cooley states that "a social self of this sort might be called the reflected or looking-glass self."[30] The self evolves as new circumstances, situations, and associations with others come into play: "People act according to their interpretation of these events, the way they see themselves, and the way they think others will react to them."[31] Therefore, until former addicts are formally and symbolically recognized as "success stories,"[32] their changes may remain suspect to significant others and to themselves. In other words, participants had not only to trust themselves but trust that significant others would eventually trust them, as well.

Participants' descriptions of new selves and new identities showed that they were starting to feel more positive about themselves. Such positive feelings included feeling good about oneself, being honest, being self-confident, and having increased self-esteem. For example, Ann talked about how she was starting to feel good about herself as she discovered, like a "baby," that there was a different world out there:

> I started to feel good about myself. Actually, I mean, I realized about myself, 'cause I looked in the mirror and I noticed that I have changed. I felt better; I'm not looking in the mirror drunk, you know. It's a whole different world there, I mean, I actually felt like, you know, this is your first new time, like, you're a baby, and you know how babies start out. You're a baby, you're starting out not drinking, you know, like, you're doing great.

Grace highlights how she was affected as she entered recovery:

> I feel confident, you know. I got a lot of confidence now. I have lot of self-esteem. I mean, I feel, I feel totally a thousand times better about myself. It [recovery] gives me a different, a different point of view of life. It gives me a different point of view. I feel like a 100 percent different person. I was different, a whole lot different from that person who was drinking. It's a big change.

Another key part of recovery for some participants was honesty with themselves. Pat suggested that this was key to her change:

> Q: Did your identity change in recovery?
> Pat: Absolutely, absolutely. It's like all the character defects face you. It's like, who am I? It's not forgetting, not regretting the past and they [AA] talk about honesty and your being honest with yourself.

Four participants talked about being honest with themselves as they narrated their recovery processes. Such self-reflection, it is argued, is key to recovery.[33] Mead argues that an individual is "fundamentally a reflective creature."[34] Once addicts fully recover, they are able to look back on their experiences as former addicts and find a "center"[35] to their lives that was not previously present. The significance of these key experiences lies in the fact that they revealed to participants something about their situations, how they felt about themselves, and the sort of people they had become.[36]

For example, as Martha explained the changes in herself, she did so using a dream metaphor. She described addiction as her "purgatory" and the following situation that occurred in her dream as a "divine intervention." As she talked to her dog, Scarlet, she recounted how this occurrence affected her:

> I go to sleep or so I thought I went to sleep. But when I really roused myself and was sitting up on the side of the bed and I know I was awake because I was petting my Doberman, and I'm sitting there talking to her and all of a sudden the room, I—this was in the middle of the night, like a Saturday night or something and I know I'm planning on getting up and going to church—there was this voice all of a sudden. Very scary, but this time I'm sitting on the edge of the bed and I'm talking to my dog. Her name is Scarlet. I said, "Scarlet, I got to quit. I'm not going to drink anymore. I have to quit. I'm having a rough time taking care of myself and I think I'll go to treatment." Now I had been going to a counselor and she kept suggesting going to treatment so I said: "I'm going to treatment, Scarlet."

Martha went on to describe the scene in her dream:

> Well, all of a sudden there's other voices in the room and over here was this man sitting on one side of my dresser looking at me and he was all in black and on the other side of the mirror was this man in white and I looked and I thought, "My God, he's in my house." So I'm holding onto the dog. She doesn't do anything, so I know I'm either dreaming or this is a hallucination. The man in black kept telling me, "She's not worth anything. Let me have her. I can bring her out of it. Let me have her." And the other person said, "No, you're wrong. There's still good in her and I'm going to help her and you can't have her." "Oh, but she drinks too much. She's not even a good mother anymore. She's not even a good worker. She's trash now. Let me have her," and the person said, "No. I told you no. I mean no. I'm

> going to keep her and tomorrow she's going to church and you can't get to her."

As she continued, Martha argued that these individuals were at odds over their rights to her:

> Now, to me, that was the devil and this was God, and so I sat there for a long time and I looked at Scarlet and I said, "Okay, baby, we can do this," so I went to treatment. I mean, I figured if the devil was talking about it, how worthless I was and that I'd never, never get over it. I thought, "You son of a bitch. I can get over it. I'm going to do it."

As Martha continued to talk about her "intervention," I asked her, "Was this the key thing that made you go into recovery?" She answered, "Yes, because when I drank, I felt worthless, just exactly the way this devil described me." For Martha, as with other participants, self-reflection was a necessary component that impelled her into recovery.

Similar to Martha's story was Phoebe's discussion of two episodes in her life that affected her decision to quit using. Phoebe had isolated herself in the woods in order to drink herself "to death." She talked about hearing voices:

> This may sound weird but during this period of time, and I'm not one to dream much or even remember them, maybe just bits and pieces. But I was in bed and I could see and hear them but I couldn't speak and they were talking about me and my life choice. They said, "Oh, it's just Phoebe. Look what she's doing to herself." And that woke me up. That [episode] had a lot of bearing on my decision [to quit].

Phoebe related how, at another time when she was isolated, she saw "a woman come down the driveway in an old car." She continued her narrative:

> A little teeny-tiny old lady and it's a cold winter's day and she's got her scarf and an old dress coat on and I'm isolated. So I go to the sun porch and she comes to the door, and she says, "God sent me here." And I said, "I beg your pardon." She said, "God sent me here." I was contemplating drinking because I wished I was dead. I was very sick and I didn't know anybody. I didn't communicate or associate with anybody and God sent her to my home. Chill bumps come up on me. She said, "You're very sick and you've been looking for something that you can't find. You have to find it for yourself and he sent me here to pray for you." I prayed with her. I allowed her to pray with me. And like I said, "I don't do organized religion. I have my convictions and my spirituality." There she was out of the blue. I have never seen her since. That was an odd experience for me.

Two other participants, Ann and Shirley, also had dreams that were factors that instigated their changes into recovery. Ann related that "I had a dream, like walking down an aisle and I seen a casket laying there. And I looked in this casket and I'm seeing myself and that's scary. So, it was time to quit." Shirley's dream involved her riding a bicycle, and in her dream she "throws away" her bag of drugs. She stated that this meant that "I don't have to be a slave to this stuff, and I'm gaining the power to be able to put it away."

Many participants mentioned prayer as a component in recovery. Prayer was an institutional, structural, or acceptable way for individuals to talk to themselves. In prayer, they reflected and contemplated, and it was this self-reflection that brought self-knowledge and allowed self changes to occur. As Kathleen noted: "I began praying. I had a reawakening in my faith, a belief that there is a higher power."

Participants were reconnecting to original selves in many cases. As women talked about their actions in *The Aware Self* phase, it was obvious that this encompassed turning points in their lives. No matter what other changes seemingly occurred, their selves had to change in order for them to see a possibility of nonaddicted selves. Aware selves that reconnected them to caring for themselves were necessary components for participants to recover.

Women's Disconnection from Using Friends and Connection with Nonusing Friends

All but three participants (who used in isolation) talked about disconnecting from using friends. Not one participant found this easy. In fact, for many, it was extremely difficult for them to push using friends away and no longer to have anything to do with them. But, as Mary stated, this was a necessary action, because she could not trust herself around them:

> Well, at first, I didn't even want to be around any people because I didn't trust anybody. I felt like any people that I think don't do it may do it, and I don't even want to risk being around people [who might be using]. I had to break off ties with my using friends and that was really hard cause I'd been friends with them and had fun with them and I really cared about them. But when it came right down to it, really all they cared about was drinking.

Theresa commented on her actions toward former using friends: "I just had to push the bad group that I had been friends with out of my life, the bad group. I don't want anything to do with you guys anymore, I told them that. I said, 'Stay away from me.'" Phoebe also observed how she began to lose her many using friends:

> I lost a lot of friends. They go drink. They would rather be with people who drink. They would rather go out on the weekends than come to my house or go to the mall. They would rather go out and dance, drink, and carry on and that changed [for me]. So, they quit coming around.

Phoebe was making the point that it was not her rejection of former using friends, but their rejection of her that enabled her to disconnect from them. On the optimistic side, participants stated that after leaving using friends, it was possible to make new ones, friends that did not use.

New friends and new relationships were necessary components in recovery because they provided positive reinforcement.[37] Without new friends, problems could arise. Without an alternative network of nonusers, the recovering addict could find herself devoid of friends and social contacts. Without friends, efforts to quit would be made much more difficult and could contribute to the recovering addict deciding to take up alcohol and/or drugs again.

New friends and/or relationships also helped to fill the social and occupational vacuum created by giving up alcohol and/or drugs. This was an essential component of any attempt to build and sustain new identities. Alternative lifestyles, which helped addicts experience themselves differently, had to be provided. Coupled with this was the necessity of a sense of purpose, a positive sense of themselves, and a stake in the future.[38]

The three participants who had used in isolation also began to make or change friends. For example, Martha commented on her tentative actions to reconnect herself to a group of friends: "Anyway, I started going out more. Like I will call a friend and say, 'Let's go out for dinner. Let's go to this new place that opened up in town.'"

Sandy, who used only with her family, managed not to "go around any of them" as she began recovery. She also commented that she still does not see her family. And Carol managed to "kick" all of her using friends out of her life.

Avoiding friends who used alcohol and/or drugs removed participants from alcohol and/or drug cultures in which they had been ensconced. Whether it was through rejecting former using friends or through making new friends in their communities, participants were aware that they needed to create new social connections to initiate recovery. Not only were they aware of changing selves in this phase, but they also were aware of the actions they needed to take in order to begin recovery.

The foregoing discussion has considered participants' awareness of their needs to construct alternative selves or to restructure their selves as they began journeys into recovery. As participants did so, they were able to engage with new social others. New social worlds and new situations provided them with feelings of connection or "embeddedness"[39] with nonaddicts and into nonaddictive lifestyles.

The following section highlights women's processes of practicing alternative selves. They began to strategize by attending AA and/or NA, acquiring a counselor, and/or entering therapy in order to deal with past physical and sexual abuse. Some participants moved away from the areas where they once used. Many began to cement relationships with nonusing friends. Others began new partner relationships. Along with structure in their lives, participants also experienced more self-control coupled with feelings of empowerment. Overall, they began to redefine experiences with alcohol and/or drugs and relationships to themselves.

The Strategic Self

> I started going back to school. I made new friends. I really changed my environment; I didn't hang out with people I was hanging out with before. I wasn't partying with them, I was working out, I stopped going to bars and doing drugs. I go backpacking, I used to go backpacking as much as I could. I moved here and bought a farm. That satisfies my need to be in nature. I'm really happy being on my own. (Rivka)

The previous section has provided a consideration of participants' awareness of their need to restructure alternative selves and social identities as they began their journeys into recovery. As participants became aware of alternative selves, identities began to change. They started to feel "different" toward themselves and started to process changes to bring them into recovery. The purpose in this section is to explore and analyze how participants strategize and practiced alternative individual and social selves. As previously stated, strategies are defined as a process of creating new social environments and new courses of action, a process of forging new social bonds and social structures in order to help participants depart from previous habits of using alcohol and/or drugs.

As Rivka stated above, participants actively strategized ways to create nonaddictive social environments within a nonaddictive social world. The women worked at creating alternative activities, such as making new friends, getting new jobs, giving "back to the community," and avoiding addictive environments (some through help in AA and/or NA). Participants built structures through new relationships in the community, attending church, and volunteering at varying agencies in their communities. While specifics varied, the women strategized to create sober social environments and sober social worlds in order to change their lives.

By creating new social environments and new courses of action in their lives, these women forged new social bonds and social structures that helped them depart from previous habits of using alcohol and/or drugs. I argue that participants' ongoing recovery consisted of strategies or "contexts of action,"[40] which incorporated both changes in themselves and changes in communities in which they were involved. Both these alterations enabled them to relinquish addictions. In developing social agency, then, these women were strategic actors and their behavior can "be interpreted to represent a dynamically adaptive process."[41]

The following three characteristics emerged in analyzing how participants told their stories of recovery: (1) Strategies such as membership in AA and/or NA were common for most participants as they struggled to stay sober. Some women also had counseling and/or sponsors to help them. Others made geographical moves away from former communities where they had used alcohol and/or drugs in order to facilitate recovery. (2) Rebuilding structure was salient for participants, as well, as they entered into a sober social world. This rebuilding of structure entailed alternate activities that participants became involved in: attending church and school activities, attending a local community center, and becoming part of women's groups in their communities. Such activities helped them to reintegrate into mainstream society. (3) Twelve women dealt with relapse challenges as they struggled to stay abstinent.

Once participants became aware of the need to activate recovery, then, they had to strategize to put it in place. In this study, strategies reflected the conscious activities participants were engaged in as they broke away from addiction and were necessary components in their recovery.[42]

Whereas changes in individual and social identities were highlighted in the first phase of recovery processes, in *The Strategic Self* phase, participants were acting to keep changes in place. The following self-descriptors were common in participants' narratives in this phase: "working the twelve steps in AA," "support is key," "counseling help," "having a good sponsor," and "making new friends." Other comments included activities that encompassed geographical moves away from former drug-using communities: "I changed my environment" and "I needed to move, that made a big difference."

Women Activating Strategies for Change

Membership in AA was a common strategy for fifteen participants as they struggled to stay sober. Two women, who were addicted to cocaine, availed themselves of NA, while one woman had memberships in both AA and NA. The women talked in interviews about the importance of their attendance at these organizations. As they talked, they were adamant about how important this was in their lives; in fact, they stressed several times how valuable these activities were and still are for them. They were talking about the help they received through membership in AA and/or NA in a way that was similar to how they originally had described how alcohol and/or drugs made them feel when addicted: that is, they were very intense in how they described their feelings. Perhaps this was because they originally had found a purpose in alcohol and/or drug use and now they were finding a similar purpose in recovery but, obviously, under different circumstances.

As fifteen participants related, AA support was key to strategizing recovery. Participants stated that it was hard work and something that they had to do to "work" their recovery. For example, Sally underscored her support through AA: "I work the program generally four times a week. I will always have to go to meetings. I will always have to work the steps. I will always have to work a proven method of recovery."

Shirley also stressed how she managed to attend AA five times a week and how all her friends were in recovery:

> I usually make on average, five meetings [AA] a week. All my friends are in AA. All my friends are in recovery. They are the only people I hang out with. Their support and love is what I received in the program. People like me have a God-sized hole in their soul.

> Have you ever heard that before? Yeah, and what fills that up is God, and, uh-huh, prayer and the people in AA, the love and support of the program. The support that I've gotten from those people [in AA] is like nothing I've ever known in my life.

The help some participants were receiving in AA was teaching them how to live relatively "normal" lives. As they strategized recovery, participants realized the importance of families, friends, children, and partners, but it seemed that their relationships and activities within AA had the most influence. Relationships with this organization provided participants with the chance to improve themselves by helping them become individuals that now could begin to relate to significant others in a non-addictive world. For example, Robbie illuminated the importance of her awareness in knowing what she "had to do" in order to activate recovery: "I never did not one of the steps [in AA]. I never made any changes in my life; I never did any of that because I thought it was a good idea. It was always because I wanted to go to AA more than I didn't want to go so I knew there were things that I had to do."

Kathleen also highlighted the importance of AA meetings for her recovery: "After going to AA, I never slipped. I never stopped and I've gone to AA ever since."

For Rhonda, "lots of meetings" provided her with a successful strategy as she began to recover: "I go to meetings, lots of meetings, working the steps, calling people. Read the Big Book [in AA]. There's all kinds of material to read."

Ten women also had counseling and/or sponsors to help them in recovery processes. For example, Tracy talked about working her program "four times a week" and having a capable sponsor. She commented on how she was beginning to strengthen her recovery:

> I went to AA and NA meetings, working the twelve steps, praying, having a good sponsor, doing all the things that were suggested to me by those members who I had seen having a significant clean time and having significant changes in their lives. It's being in daily contact with other addicts, it's making a decision to have recovery over getting high.

Marie found that both her sponsor and AA provided her the help she needed:

> There are all kinds of different groups, and you have to pick and choose the groups that are right for you and if you use them for what they're for, they're very helpful and that's where I found my sponsor actually and I had a really strong home group in AA. So I think they're very beneficial.

Nancy's structure and support was with a sponsor and a therapist, along with her many weekly meetings at AA:

> I had help, yeah, I had help. I mean between going into, going into therapy and my sponsor in AA, this has been very important. I go to AA at least five times a week. I know that I need four or five meetings [AA] a week. It's part of my structure, it's part of my daily structure.

Perhaps participants' self changes could not have happened in isolation. Perhaps they could. But if an individual did recover without any help whatsoever, it might take longer or might not last. As many participants stated, help within memberships at AA and/or NA was giving them proper tools to assimilate themselves into a new social world that included new associations, new and necessary structure, support, knowledge about addiction and recovery, love, the opportunity to relinquish old ways of thinking, and a commitment to something besides alcohol and/or drugs. AA and/or NA provided them with an extended family that, as many participants stated, "cared" about them and the fact that they stayed sober.

Deb's strategies were with both AA and NA. In particular, they provided her with what she termed her "extended family" and gave her needed support: "It is also great to have that sort of extended family that has that problem. That has had an addiction that can help you through it. You need lots of support. You need people constantly telling you, 'You can do it. You can do it.'"

Drug counseling, along with membership in AA, was an important strategy for several participants. Sandy highlighted this strategy: "Normally, I'm either in a group of AA or counseling or I work. I have a therapist, I do my drug counseling."

Pat also contributed her insights into her particular strategy:

> My children's grandmother is a counselor, and I was going to AA and picnics and enjoying the fellowship with her. I started going to meetings like three or four a week. Then, I started going to an outpatient group for outpatient addicts at the health department. I started getting some, some knowledge about the disease, and learning how to talk in a group and then I got a parenting counselor through addiction.

The following table highlights the overall institutional and community support that participants took advantage of as they began recovery.

Table 4.1. Types of Institutional and Community Support

Types of Support	Frequency percent	(n)
AA /NA	68.0	(17)
None	32.0	(8)
Total:	100.0	(25)

Seventeen participants used institutional help in recovery, such as AA or NA, while the remaining women (n=8) recovered without institutional help. The eight participants who self-recovered stated that they found these organizations oppressive or not to their liking, or they stated that they did not need such support. Of these eight, seven did not have any counseling during recovery. They stated that friends, boyfriends, church members, and/or husbands provided their main support. Moreover, these participants did not seem to find it any more difficult or any easier to process their recovery than did the seventeen who had institutional support.

The women who recovered without institutional help were clear about what other types of support they needed. For example, Grace mentioned the help she received from her husband and mother: "Well, my husband helped me and then when my mum realized what, what I was going through, she, she kinda helped me a little bit too. She would, you know, understand the issue and keep my kids for me. You know, every, just every once in awhile she'd keep my kids for me."

Susan depended on her husband and parents for her support as well. She attended AA for a month or so, but then decided it was not for her. When I asked her, "So, why didn't you go to AA? Why didn't it work for you?" she answered:

> I guess that AA works, it's just, once you feel you don't need them, you shouldn't go back. I mean you get to the point where you feel uncomfortable, or you feel like you're saying the same things over and over because they're asking you the same things over and over, then it's time not to go back.

Betty, too, depended on her mother for support when she decided to leave the addictive lifestyle. One participant, Hannah, did not know about AA and/or NA at all: "I wasn't really aware of it [AA]." Another participant, Rivka, went to one AA meeting, then did not go back because she found it too oppressive:

> I tried to go to an AA meeting and I just found it so oppressive. There's something about the conformity of everybody standing up and saying, "Hi, my name is blah, blah, and I'm an alcoholic." And I also didn't like the idea of continuing to identify myself as an alcoholic and saying you're an alcoholic your whole life. I just thought there was something wrong with that and I never went back.

Esther, who was coerced into recovery after her conviction for manufacturing Ecstasy, was extremely angry that she had to attend Health Recovery Services (HRS) as a condition of her probation. She was adamant about not attending NA:

> Q: Have you ever tried NA?
> Esther: No, and I thank God that I don't have to go to that. No, because I don't want to surround myself with those people and the addicts and the stories. You know, I'll go and see my probation officer, but I'm really angry that they're making me go to these meetings [at HRS].

Despite these exceptions, most participants relied on institutional support as they began recovery. Self-help groups, such as AA and/or NA, dramatically reoriented some participants' meanings toward alcohol and/or drugs and provided them with alternative communities that socialized them into lifestyles of recovery.[43]

Geographical Moves as a Strategy for Change

> I felt if I didn't move, I wasn't going to make it. There was just no question. I can't be around these people [her former using friends]. I'm not going to make it if I am going to be around these people, so I had to move, you know, move someplace where I didn't know anybody. (Hannah)

Breaking one's ties to the alcohol and/or drug scene often requires relocation. Such physical relocation is referred to as a "geographic cure."[44] Relocation serves to remove women from the alcohol and/or drug culture in which they had been embedded. Maruna[45] suggests that the "geographic cure" may be part of how addicts manage to desist when they move away from former using neighborhoods. It might be one way for addicts to understand that addiction was outside of their control.

Such cures were effective as a means of removing participants from a network of alcohol and/or drug users. Eight participants made such a move. Of the eight participants who did not avail themselves of institutional help such as AA and/or NA, only two of them made a geographical move away from where they formerly had used. The following table highlights these two groups:

Table 4.2. Geographical Moves

Geographical moves	Frequency percent	(n)
Yes	32.0	(8)
No	68.0	(17)
Total:	100.0	(25)

Mary had lived several years in New York City. Her time there was difficult. It was where she had prostituted for a time and where she had become a mother to two children. Finally, when she became pregnant with her third child, she realized that she needed to move away from her addictive community in order to provide some sense of normal life for her children. Thus, she decided to move "back home." She explained her move from New York and stressed the importance of not moving back there: "It was kind of like I just knew, don't go back to New York. I just kept telling myself, don't go back."

Pat was also very cognizant of the importance of moving away from areas where she formerly had used alcohol and/or drugs: "I moved a few times in the last couple of years. I moved into a new town so I didn't know very many people." Linda too stated that

> I moved out of the county. That made a big difference, too, because all my friends and my social group were here, you know, the same people I had been drinking with for the last twelve years or so. I moved north, north of here and that made a difference because I think I got out, away from the group. It was easier for me.

In this phase, participants were using particular strategies to activate recovery. Whether it was through institutional help or help from friends, family, and/or partners, or whether a geographical move was necessary, participants were keenly aware that they had to actively create new social connections that would help them end their addictions. Such variations suggested that cessation experiences were similar in many respects for participants and that whatever actions participants took, they worked for them.

Women Rebuilding Structure in the Community

As these women strategized to recover, they signified that they also had to rebuild structure in their lives as they entered into sober social worlds. Women recognized that they needed alternative activities as necessary components for recovery. Such activities helped them reintegrate into mainstream society. Participants did this in several ways: through involvement in church and school activities, by attending local community centers, and by becoming part of local women's groups. The following table highlights these activities for participants as they strategize recovery.

Table 4.3. Community Activities

Type	Frequency percent	(n)
Church	16.0	(4)
School	24.0	(6)
Community center	16.0	(4)
Women's groups	8.0	(2)
Total:	64.0	(16)

Church, School, and Community Activities

Four participants mentioned church as an important part of recovery. Church, they suggested, provided them with a sense of community in conventional society. For example, Ann stressed the importance of it in her life: "My son and I went to church. We started going to the churches, talked to other people who went to church, I had the preachers come to my house."

When Hannah was younger, church life had been very important to her. She said, "I went to church when I was a kid, a little girl and, in fact, I used to love to go to church." In her addiction, she completely "turned away" from her former religious beliefs and did not attend at all. However, in her recovery, she realized that church again had to be an important part of her life. Thus, she returned, and, as she stated: "I am also active in my church. I counsel people, I talk to them, you know, so I give back to people."

Returning to school was a factor for six of the participants as they began recovery and as they strategized to stay abstinent. Some attended a local community college, while others completed university degrees. For example, for Nancy, after she became sober, school became an important factor in her life: "I went to school and I took all classes. I went to [the local] college and then I went back and got my bachelor's [degree]."

Pat, too, related her accomplishments at university: "After I got sober, I went to school. I got an associate's degree in business. I went back to school and got my master's degree. No one in my family had ever gone on to school."

Two other women, Linda and Marie, also attended the local university in order to "get an education." For Linda, in particular, this was an accomplishment that "got her a better job." And Marie received her bachelor's degree in 2000, something she is very proud of.

Participants were also rebuilding structure in their personal lives. Martha, for example, intentionally planned her day so she was constantly busy:

> It was not easy to not have the companionship of that bottle. It was hard to go from work on Friday night and so what I would do, I'd come home; I'd probably change clothes because I tried to dress up very nicely at work. I would come home. I would change clothes. I would go in, I would find an excuse to go to town. Maybe go get something to eat and then go to an AA meeting. On Saturday night, a lot of times it would be church because we have a Saturday night Mass. Sundays, if I could go to church on Saturday night, then Sunday morning, if it was going to be a pretty day, then I'm working around the log cabin. I go outdoors the minute it gets daylight.

A community center had been active in the region where the study took place for several years and was sponsored by a city organization. It was open very early in the morning and late at night and several participants (n=4) spent their days there interacting with other women, similar to Ann's experience:

> I pushed my using friends away from me. So I don't have so very many friends anymore except at the Community Center. I made quite a few friends—the whole Community Center people. Everybody comes there; we've all become friends. The Community Center is helping me a lot.

Dealing with Relapse Challenges

A prominent occurrence, as some researchers suggest,[46] in former addicts' lives is their experiences of relapse. Relapse is defined as a period of time in which addicts return to their alcohol and/or drug use before reentering recovery once again. Relapse remains the rule rather than the exception when it comes to solving problems.[47] Arguing that a linear progression of change is possible but relatively rare, Prochaska et al.[48] maintain that most individuals wishing to change may "go around in circles" three or four times before they finally exit previous habits. A vast majority of relapsers internalize the lessons they learn from previous efforts and eventually give up their habits altogether.[49]

Twelve participants in this study also followed this route. Although it may seem that relapsing is not what could be called, a strategy, the participants clarified the fact that relapsing enabled them to learn how to strategize as Prochaska et al.[50] suggest so as not to reenter addiction and to continue on into their recovery. Of these, the average number of relapses was between one and three, while one participant relapsed five times before she finally terminated her addiction. The following table shows the number of relapses for participants.

Table 4.4. Participants' Relapses

No. of Relapses	Frequency Percent	(n)
1–3	44.0	(11)
4+	4.0	(1)
Total:	48.0	(12)

One participant, Nancy, started drinking again when she stopped going to AA meetings. She had convinced herself, for a time, that she was not an alcoholic. After she returned to attending weekly meetings, she stated: "I don't want to do that again [using alcohol], because I did do that before. I stopped going to meetings. I think that's crucial, just for me, you know."

Robbie, who had been abstinent for eighteen years, commented that she did not know there was such a thing as relapse: "I didn't even know I could for the longest time. I didn't know you could drink and go back. I'd never heard that. I was well over three months [in recovery] before I heard [that] and I was like, why would you want to do that?"

Sally, too, relapsed, but her reason for doing so related to how she met her husband. When I asked her if she ever had relapsed, she stated, "Once. That was the night that I got drunk with my husband. When we went out to dinner, that's how he convinced me to go out with him." When I asked how she felt about relapsing, she responded, "It felt good because I met him, but it felt really bad in the morning. I mean, a 'mondo' hangover. And really sick because after you don't drink for all that time, you get really, immensely sick."

Another participant, Ann, who initially had become addicted to alcohol when she was in her teens as a result of her marriage to a sixty-two-year-old man, managed to quit her use at age sixteen with her father's help: "My dad helped me get off [the alcohol] when I was about sixteen." However, her father's death, which affected her very deeply, compelled her to begin using again for a period of seven years until she entered recovery at age thirty-seven. She stated that, upon her father's death, "I started back up again, and I didn't quit."

Hannah, too, experienced two relapses when she was in recovery from her marijuana use: "Maybe two major relapses. Like I said before, I would smoke every day, all day. But then it would be like I would go three or four months, five months, I wouldn't smoke and then I would go a couple more."

Two other participants, Sandy and Rivka, relapsed only "one or two times" before they established themselves in recovery processes. For Marie, although she never relapsed, one time it was a "'close thing." This occurrence also cemented her not "hanging with" such friends anymore:

> No, but I have been close [to relapsing]. I got back with some of my old buddies and they'd hand me a beer and it was so natural to just pick it up and want to drink it. I handed it back to her; I just had to, that scared me enough after working that hard, just to mess it all up. So I quit hanging with those friends and slowly have developed other friends.

Relapse is a normal and regular occurrence with those who want to change former habits. For these participants, it was a regular occurrence in some of their lives, but most importantly, such "recycling" gave them opportunities to learn. Prochaska et al.[51] refer to the term, "recycle to relapse" and argue that actions followed by relapses are far better than no actions at all.

The patterns that instigated changes in participants' lives varied in this phase, yet all participants were similar in their approaches as they attributed different meanings to themselves. Whether it was through attendance at AA and/or NA, gaining support from significant others, moving away from addictive communities, dealing with relapse challenges, or rebuilding structure through various activities, the women were redefining experiences as they strategized recovery. As they redefined experiences, participants were learning to live again.

The following section analyzes participants' stable selves. How they saw themselves as they stabilized recovery was key to understanding this process. As one participant stated, "I trust in myself now."

The Stable Self

> I trust in myself now, working the program and I, I just don't have anything in my system. I believe in my instincts, you know, and like when I feel pain or fear and stuff, I thank God. My job is to like listen to that and kind of act appropriately and accordingly as I'm weaving through life. (Carol)

I began this chapter with a discussion of how participants became aware of how individual and social selves were in need of change in order for recovery to begin. As this awareness progressed, the women began to define, through various actions, the strategies they needed to put in place in order to become stable in abstinence. Thus far, I have discussed two phases leading to participants' recovery: *The Aware Self* and *The Strategic Self*. These two phases prepared participants for stabilizing their lives as they further cemented their recovery processes.

In this section, I discuss the final phase of ongoing recovery for participants: *The Stable Self* phase. This section shows how participants exercised and stabilized alternative lives for themselves in recovery processes. In addition to considering important others in their lives, these women exercised plans for their futures and strived for new relationships. They were more recovered than addicted. Even though the balance had shifted, struggles persisted. They talked about ongoing challenges in recovery and the difficulties that existed as they struggled to maintain abstinence.

As women talked about this phase, they mentioned how involved they were in volunteer work in their communities, activities they talked about with great pride. Volunteering seemed to be a very necessary and significant component in these women's recovery. They reveled in this new pursuit. It seemed that this level of attachment to and involvement in volunteering gave them benefits that went along with the transformation of their selves in recovery. Such activity allowed participants to "live with the world as opposed to against and above it."[52] Perhaps, in a real sense, this activity represented an investment in healthy social relationships that provided them much happiness and satisfaction with recovered selves. In order to fully recover, participants needed "not only motive, but also method."[53]

Method, then, was giving back to the community. Participants had been introduced to more than one option and, as a consequence, they chose not to go back to the devil they knew.[54] I argue that, as well, volunteering was a type of rehabilitative therapy for participants and was empowering. Whitmore argues "people will change simply by 'doing' for somebody else."[55]

One of the major characteristics in this phase of participants' recovery processes was the stability that existed for most of the women. When talking about addiction, the women consistently were sad and despondent. In contrast, as they talked about recovery, their voices and even their body language changed. They were dynamic and happy as they discussed their ongoing stability and the actions they had initiated in new lives. Participants were consistent in mentioning activities such as work, involvement with others, and continuing education that assisted them in reinforcing restructured selves.

I documented six emergent key characteristics that constituted or ensured stability in this phase of participants' lives: (1) Stable selves and identities were consistent for all participants in activities in the social world in which they now were constantly involved. Such activities provided participants with a strong sense of self. The most important factor was involvement with significant others who reinforced restructured selves. (2) Along with stable selves and identities came resultant actions that provided participants stability in recovering lives, that is, work and continuing education. (3) Continuing institutional and personal support was key for all the women. (4) A key element in recovery was active work at producing good relationships in recovery processes, that is, volunteering and helping others in their communities. All participants mentioned this sense of community as a necessary element as they cemented their recovery; a sense of "giving back" was prominent in their lives. (5) Participants mentioned present and future plans as ones filled with hopes, fun, and pleasure. (6) Finally, the women were very cognizant of struggles and dilemmas in abstinence.

Participants described this phase of recovery in terms of happiness, normalcy, plans for new lives, sociability, loving relationships, self-esteem, along with descriptions of how difficult recovery processes had been. It was obvious that behaviors had changed. They were now considering others. They were helpful to others who were still addicted, and they believed that they needed to be active in their communities. They were planning for new futures and new lives, beginning new relationships, cementing previous relationships with significant others, working, continuing their education, and were being financially responsible. Still, struggles persisted, and they still dealt with dilemmas in recovery processes.

The Beginning of Stable Selves

Participants talked about how their lives, as well as how their individual selves and identities had changed as they stabilized recovery processes. For example, all the women related that they had changed in some manner. They were happy with the activities they were involved in as they reported that they just felt good about themselves.

I heard common words that obviously were consequences of recovery: "happy," "enjoy," "feeling different about self," "feeling better about self," and increased self-esteem. In this phase, participants were constructing different meanings toward themselves and toward others. For example, Carol highlights these feelings: "You know I feel perfectly fine about myself and I don't need to drink 100 beers because I'm so unhappy with the way things are. And I don't care about what anybody thinks any more. Just me and my girls, they're happy, I'm happy, and vice versa, you know."

For Deb it was finding enjoyment in her life: "And, you know, and, you know, I think it was just, you know, that transition for me, just finding my way again of what I enjoyed."

Esther, who now had a regular schedule in her life, stated, "I'm really feeling good about myself and they like me at home and I enjoy the girls I work with." Betty's story was similar as she processed recovery: "I felt different about myself, healthier. And I quit smoking too. I felt stable in life, that's for sure."

Carol talked about how her image of herself had changed and about how recovery had made her a stronger woman, able to cope better with life's problems. Grace, too, stated that she saw herself as a "100 percent different person," from the one she had been when she used alcohol and drugs. She now was getting "high on life" and felt "totally a thousand times better about myself."

And Sandy highlighted how she felt in control of her life:

> I think I will be successful because I am taking control of my life. I am learning to stand on my own two feet. I am thirty-four, and I am just learning to do the things most seventeen- and eighteen-year-olds

> are learning to do at the same time right now, you know. I am filling out job applications, learning how to drive, learning how to pump gas, um, learning my way around, all that.

Among some participants, the word "control" had a strong meaning. Although they felt in control of their lives and their selves, what they did to increase such feelings related to individual strengths gained by putting themselves in situations where they had control, that is, work, school, community activities, and so on. Participants were working at getting control in their lives. As Phoebe states: "I'm in charge of my life. I have taken control and I like being in control. I've taken my life back. I'm not chained to a beer can or a whiskey bottle [anymore]."

The move from addiction to abstinence requires fundamental changes in the central premise of control.[56] Brown argues "the individual shifts from a belief in self-control to a recognition of loss of control."[57] As addicts became addicted, they lost control over their usage of substances. Ultimately, as they gained back control of their selves, participants also gained a sense of control over their use of alcohol and/or drugs.

Women's Stable Behaviors: Work and School

In recovery, seven participants began working, and six were either attending school or had plans to do so in the near future.

Table 4.5. Work and School Activities

Activities	Frequency Percent	(n)
Work	28.0	(7)
Higher education	24.0	(6)
Total:	52.0	(13)

Phoebe became a county service worker in a group home for the mentally challenged and disabled, a job that she "loves" to do: "I'm a county service worker—I work in group homes for the mentally challenged and disabled. I work with some pretty serious folks and I love it. It's a humbling experience."

Martha volunteers at the Rehabilitation Services Commission, helps to organize the Consumer Advocacy Council in her community, and works with women who are addicted.

Nancy highlighted her working life: "I have a very simple job; I just do customer's services at Good Food Direct Co-op." Deb, too, stated: "In my job I first started out working with the adult population in Health Recovery Services. Then I got the offer to work on the kid's team and I thought, okay, I'll try it."

Hannah reiterated the importance of living a normal life that she finds "totally different":

> I also decided it was time to get a job. So I went and got a job in a fast food restaurant. I remember thinking that I hadn't worked at a fast food restaurant since I was fifteen years old. I now operated in the daytime because I was a night person. I get up at eight in the morning and get ready and I go to work. I come home and enjoy some dinner, you know, leisure activities. It's just totally different.

Marie became an entrepreneur and decided to run for political office in her community: "I started my own paper; I started networking with all kinds of small businesses. And then I actually ran for township trustee two years ago."

Six participants who had been stable in recovery for several years went back to school. Two women fairly new in recovery were either attending school or had plans to do so in the near future. For example, both Shirley and Lynn attended the local university, working toward their degrees. Other women were planning on continuing their education. For Nancy, this was an important goal in her abstinence: "What I am looking forward to is school. A degree in communications and a broadcast journalist is what I want to do. I did nothing before, but everyday now, I do something and it's different everyday."

Theresa, too, planned on attending community college in the near future in order to "take nursing." And Pat was quite adamant about her future as she planned to enter the counseling field: "I want to do parenting counseling. I will start this winter. Now I feel very settled. I'm very gratified. I feel happy within myself." Sandy's dream was to get her GED and then to work with women in recovery: "Either I want to work there or I want to go a little bit further and be a drug counselor or something like that."

Work and school provided stability in participants' lives in this phase and gave the women a sense of purpose and a sense of empowerment. Empowerment is about "learning through doing,"[58] and such accomplishments increased participants' sense of self-efficacy. Work and school were rewarding activities for participants; they provided support, enabling these women to desist from using alcohol and/or drugs.

Receiving Institutional and Personal Support

Despite activity and immersion within communities, seventeen participants were still aware of practicing strategies in "new" lives in order to keep "new" selves in line. The following table highlights support systems for participants. Numbers overlap because some participants availed themselves of both institutional help, such as AA and/or NA, along with counseling and family support.

Table 4.6. Continuing Support in Recovery

Types of Support	Frequency Percent	(n)
Institutional support	68.0	(17)
Counseling	28.0	(7)
Other support	12.0	(3)

These participants were still attending AA and/or NA, some at least five times a week, and continuing to cement abstinence. Seven were receiving ongoing counseling in recovery, while three were gaining support from family, friends, and/or partners or husbands.

Shirley talked about the support she received from a friend and emphasized how supportive people were in AA:

> I have a wonderful support. In fact one of my very, very close friends—they call him Miracle ____. That's one of his nicknames. He's been sober, I don't know, over ten years and he lives that extreme lifestyle I did cause it's nowhere like nowhere else in the country. Boy, one time I was ready to go out and drink. Not too long ago actually. About two months ago I just couldn't deal [with it] and ____ called me up said, "How you doing?" and I said, "I'm going to go drink." He says, "Well, why don't I come over and you can go to a [AA] meeting." That's happened to me. He's actually watching my son tonight while I go to a meeting. The support that I've gotten from these people is like nothing I've ever known in my life.

Mary attends her AA group once a week, which keeps her "connected":

> I go to group once a week. It keeps me connected and, you know, [connects] me to people that are going through the same thing and realize that it's, it's like the most highest placed group there as far as, like they just created a women in recovery group which I am in, but it's like a relapse prevention group. It's the highest place there because it's for people that are, really, they seem really dedicated to their recovery.

The role of social support from others was a key element in recovery and ongoing abstinence. Mary also has a good friend outside of AA who understands her struggles and who supports her: "I've enabled myself to get close to [her] and she totally understands my recovery. She has me and I have her and somehow we still keep ourselves out of trouble, you know."

Other participants received continuing support from partners and family members. Rhonda explained the importance of this support from her daughters and her partner. She talked about how her children provided support: "If I have a problem, I'll call one of them and they'll talk to me or take me to meetings." Her partner also provides support. The help she was receiving reaffirmed her new lifestyle, helping her to continue to lead a new alcohol-free life:

> My partner supports me, he takes me to meetings and he goes with me. He knows what I've been going through a little bit and he's learning every day, too, because he sure didn't like me the way I was. I depend on a lot of people. They pick me up. I know I have to do what is told to me. I have to read the Big Book. I have to meditate and I have to go to meetings and I have to be around clean and sober people if I want to stay clean.

Marie's support comes from friends in AA and from a personal friend whom she has known for years:

> Well, I started making friends in AA and with my sponsor and I stayed really good friends with a couple of girls who were in treatment with me. Then I had this best friend, he's been my friend since probably the '60s, he's been my constant friend and he's always been there for me.

As illustrated in the above quotes, participants were practicing strategies, thus cementing abstinence. Whether it was attending AA or NA, availing themselves of counseling, or receiving assistance from supportive families or friends, such "supporting maintenance"[59] helped women to stay "clean and sober" as they practiced addiction.

Volunteering and Helping Others

Of importance to twenty-two of the participants was "giving back" to their community. A sense of "social citizenship" was relevant in their lives. Participants found newfound pleasures in productive pursuits and expressing their attachments to particular groups, communities, or causes. The women found something that mattered to them in their lives: social purpose and meaning in "giving back" to their communities. Connections to something larger than the self are a vital part of recovery processes.[60] This was an important aspect of recovery because it helped participants "keep their sobriety." For example, Lynn says: "It's the giving back, the showing up at meetings to help the new people [in AA]. If someone new comes up, be there to help them, sponsor someone. Help someone. You won't be able to keep your sobriety if you don't."

Martha emphasized that she is now a more "outgoing person" which enables her to provide support to other members of AA and to help other women who are now in jail. The fact that Martha is more "outgoing" in her life makes it possible for her to help others:

> You're more of an outgoing person [in recovery] because you're happy within yourself and so, I go to an AA meeting and I see some poor soul sitting there like this. I'll go over and say, "Hi, my name's Martha, how are you doing today?" I go up to the local jail. It's a three-county jail. I go up there every Wednesday night and we have an AA meeting with the women.

Kathleen is helping to build houses for Habitat for Humanity, as well as volunteering on the American Cancer Society Board and the AIDS Task Force. She continues to expand on her volunteering and activity within her community:

> I've been very active and I've always got something going on. I think the first thing I did around that time was I became a hospice volunteer. I was always doing, I did a lot of volunteer stuff over the years. I

> had more of a sense of giving back, more of a sense of, I, one of the little things I like which I think I first heard at a meeting was, ah, how does it go? Life is God's gift to you. What you do with your life is your gift to God. And I thought: I need to do something with my life.

Four participants are volunteers for two organizations in the community that work with women. Helping others seems to be a key element in participants' recovery: they are actively working to produce good relationships with others in a sober world. For example, Sandy is "starting another group for women," while Robbie, too, is doing counseling with former women addicts.

Many participants stipulated that AA was teaching them "to be of service." Participants took this teaching to heart, as Lynn stated: "So I spent all last summer helping people in the program. Helping them with their houses or cleaning houses. I'm on the call list, and when they need someone to talk to, someone for a twelve-step call and I take them out like once a week to go to a twelve-step meeting."

Shirley also reiterated what she does to help others: "I want to help women get through their stuff. I'm active now. I'm going to be doing the local Women's Liaison Project." For Hannah, church activities are now a constant in her life: "I am really active in my church. I counsel people, I talk to them, you know, I just. I feel such compassion for people. It's like I feel their pain. So, I give back to people and I'm finally living in a place where I feel comfortable."

Marie too "started a bible study group again and I've done that off and on for the last eight years." Rhonda, perhaps, summed it up best when she talked about all the things she is managing to do in her stable, active life:

> I meditate every morning. Go to AA, I love to garden. I've got a big garden, taking care of my plants, calling my children, taking care of my grandchildren. My life is, I'm filling it up with things that I don't have to feel guilty about the next day. Yes, you have to be back in the community, maybe do some 12-step calls if somebody is having a real hard time. Go to their house and talk to them. I have to read my Big Book. I have to meditate and I have to go to meetings and I have to be around clean and sober people if I want to stay clean. [You need to] reach out for help.

By volunteering and helping others, participants were managing recovery processes. Wanting to help others was a reciprocal gesture for participants because many had received such help themselves. These "gestures of restoration"[61] enabled participants to gain back a sense of pride and to resume self-respecting individual selves and social identities.

Women's Present and Future Plans

All participants talked about their present and future plans with joy. One woman, who owns her own farm, is working to make it profitable for herself.

Rivka explained how this environment, with help from a few of her friends, is making her life a happy and supportive one:

> I'm happiest in my life right now because I own my farm now. I think there's something really powerful about, about changing your environment, for me anyway. I'm trying to make it profitable not only to support me, but it's got to be profitable. I get a lot of help from friends, a lot, a lot of help from friends.

Kathleen, who traveled half the Appalachian Trail in her early recovery, now wants to return and complete the entire route and to continue to do "all sorts of things" in her sober life: "Oh, I have a lot of dreams. I did a backpacking trip on the Appalachian Trail. I want to take photography classes and I want to write more and I want to maybe get into breathing or meditation class. I've got all sorts of things that I want to do."

Another woman wants to stay home and raise her children well and is looking forward to being a grandparent. And Hannah is planning to go on a missionary crusade to Ethiopia with her pastor and other church members:

> I've had an invitation; actually I had an invitation to go this year to Ethiopia on a crusade, a mission crusade. My pastor has been going the last couple years. He goes a couple times a year and like 35,000 children were filled with the Holy Ghost last year under his ministry and he goes to these crusades every year and he gave me the invite.

Several participants intend to continue their education. As Theresa stated, her plans include both work and schooling. Whether she actually fulfills her dreams, her future is filled with hope: "My future plans: to get my own home, my own Ford F-150 truck. I have wanted to join the Coast Guard since I was seventeen." Shirley wants to "get my nursing degree and work and I want to get more degrees. I want to go to law school. That's what I really want to do. I want to go to law school."

Robbie, who is an artist, also wants to continue her education and "expand" her life: "I'm doing memory quilts. I'm an artist. And I want to expand. I mean I don't know. I try not to shut myself in any boxes. I would really like to try to work at the university because I would like to continue my education. I would like to go on with my education." These quotes illustrate the women's hopes and sense of optimism. Engaging in such activities, participants stated, enables them to find something of value in their lives and gives them a sense of control over their destinies. However participants see present and future plans, it is with a sense of optimism coupled with overall active lifestyles. It was obvious during the interviews that they talked about their plans as cemented within a sober social world and with clear eyes to their futures.

Women's Awareness of Continuing Struggles in Abstinence

Participants were very aware that struggles and dilemmas will persist in recovered lives, but they now had the knowledge that they need to live sober lives. Overall, participants were no longer afraid of their selves and they had more of a chance to be successful in their endeavors. For example, Theresa explained how, for her, it was going to be a constant "fight" and a long recovery:

> It's like if you are addicted once I think you are always going to be addicted. I mean, I think you may not have to fight it every day but you're going to come to times when you are going to have to fight it and I believe that, I may not desire it but who knows, I may desire it Sunday. You never know. I think that it can happen. I think it's always going to be a long recovery.

Marie talked about how she had to find other things to do when she entered recovery, things to fill the gap that her drug of choice, alcohol, used to fill: "It was so hard when I stopped drinking so I had to find other things to do. I started oil painting and I took my son to oil painting lessons."

As with most, if not all participants, feelings about substances and their understanding of their connections to their use is clarified by Robbie: "Alcohol's not my problem. It's the alcohol and me. I mean there are people that can drink a glass or two and can walk away. I have no understanding of that."

Phoebe knows what she needs to do to continue her new lifestyle and thinks this is her second chance at life, as she says:

> There are days when I wish I could be a social drinker enjoying [it with] someone for a glass of wine or stop and have a cold beer with a friend. I have a full plate right now in my private life or my personal life and there are days when I would like to throw up my hands and say, "To hell with this." I talk myself out of it; I just can't go there. I can't drink. I'm happier. I can see more clearly. It's easier. I can't explain it. I got a second chance.

Even though challenges and dilemmas persist for participants, many talked about the "joy" in recovery. For example, Nancy emphasizes this feeling in her new lifestyle:

> With all the pain, I feel as deep as that pain goes, I feel equal amounts of joy, so it's pretty cool. It's like a real peaceful feeling, like things are just as they're supposed to be, that everything is right with the world, you know. Um, that I've seen how and I know what it looks like and I don't have to look at that anymore, um, I don't know, I mean, I put the music on in my house and I dance by myself, it's just little tiny things that feel really, you know, things are okay. I never felt like things were just okay, I never did, I never felt like I am just okay, I never had it before, even the first time I recovered, I didn't have it, but I have that now.

Phoebe mentions that recovery has been a process and a journey for her; she has "taken her life back":

> My recovery is a process and it's a journey. Every day is a new experience. I've had my moments but, for the most part, it's easy. It's not a struggle like it was where you just wanted to throw in the towel and give it up. I've worked so hard and I've come so far and everyday is a new experience and now that I'm in recovery and I have a different way of thinking and it's not negative thoughts. It's more positive thoughts every day and I'm not going to allow, I'm not going to give anybody the power to make me drink.

Many participants mentioned that they were now "in control" of their lives; they were now "in charge." Overall, the women's narratives showed that their power now was greater than the power alcohol and/or drugs had had over their lives at one time. Participants, in giving up control over substances, had gained their personal power back, signifying "less a relinquishment of 'power' than a clarification of personal power's finiteness."[62]

Women's Insights into Addiction and Recovery Processes

As the interview process concluded, the women shared wonderful insights into their experiences of who they had been while in addiction and recovery. They seemingly had gained new perspectives on their selves, a sense of structured selves that gave them strength in recovery. Perspective, in this sense, refers to a coordinated set of ideas and actions participants used in dealing with recovery. It refers to the women's ways of thinking, feeling about, and acting in recovery. Their actions in recovery flowed from new beliefs in themselves, and these beliefs now justified their actions.[63]

Participants in recovery had investments in their everyday lives. Such investments often are taken for granted and rarely receive much attention.[64] These women were committed to their everyday lives. As Flacks argues:

> In addition to all those activities that are ultimately grounded in physical survival, everyday life is constituted by activity and experience designed to sustain one's self as a human being—to validate or fulfill the meaning of one's life, reinforce or enhance one's sense of self-worth, achieve satisfaction and pleasure or, negatively, to overcome distress, resolve problems, restore continuity, do duties so that the life one believes or expects one to have or to be entitled to can be lived.[65]

Personal resilience seemed to provide participants with incentives not only to change but also to continue with abstinence. The strength of these individual selves and social identities is shown in the following insights as they remembered their former selves and described and defined their present, stable lives. For example, Nancy emphasized not forgetting her former self: "I don't ever want to forget. I have enough sobriety now under my belt that I don't have the cravings, but I have the knowledge that if I don't continue going to meetings that I will forget where I came from." Carol reiterated Nancy's insights as well: "I need to be in recovery at some level for the rest of my life. To go into a meeting and to see that new woman come in, in the excruciating pain that I was in, to remind me, oh my God, that's what it was like when I first got sober. I don't want to do that again."

Mary emphasized her confidence in her new self and the knowledge of what she had learned during recovery:

> For me, it's beginning to be about taking out what I've learned through the recovery process and using it in the real world where it enriches me. It makes me feel better. When I am confident in what I am doing, when I am given the chance to talk about it like this is why I really feel confident through it because I feel like I can really go somewhere or something, finish my degree, do things I always wanted to do that I was told as a child, you can do anything you want, you can be anything you want.

And Phoebe highlighted her enjoyment of her new life: "I've come so far that it's easy for me to get up in the morning and chose not to take a drink because I like my life today. It's not the best, but it's a hell of a lot better than it was and I enjoy it and I enjoy my job. I enjoy my health."

Shirley's insights related to living sober, and also she emphasized how her recovery was and is a journey:

> Oh, I'm learning. I'm learning how to live. Not only live sober, but how to live. I never knew that. I knew how to do drugs. I knew how to be fucked up. Oh, I didn't know how to live. I didn't know how to be sober and I'm still learning about that. My recovery is a journey. It's a process. It's both a journey and a process. It's a never-ending journey.

As I listened to these women's narratives, I felt as if they had an obligation to their selves to stay clean, to stay sober. Tracy stated that she sees herself as obligated to cement her recovery: "I'm not in recovery to stay clean; I'm in recovery to become the person God intended me to become in the first place." She gave a critical view of recovery when I asked her to define it for me: "Recovery is the absence of insanity." For participants, their addiction and recovery processes had been arduous journeys, journeys of coming back from their "insanity."

Summary

Through participants' narratives, I have considered the factors that characterized these women's lives as they ended their addiction and entered recovery in this chapter. Through an analysis of women's awareness of alcohol and/or drug use, coupled with their strategic actions, I have attempted to illustrate how participants struggled to maintain stable selves. The knowledge gained through these journeys provided participants not only with new identities and new selves, but also with wisdom, which has enabled them to move forward as they constructed new lives.

Notes

1. H. Becker, "Becoming a Marijuana User," *American Journal of Sociology* 59 (1953): 235–42.
2. Becker, "Becoming a Marijuana User," 242.
3. L. Levine, *Codependent Forevermore* (Chicago: University of Chicago Press, 1999).
4. S. Brown, *Treating the Alcoholic: A Developmental Model of Recovery* (New York: John Wiley and Sons, 1985); H. R. F. Ebaugh, *Becoming an Ex: The Process of Role Exit* (Chicago: University of Chicago Press, 1988).
5. J. Hewitt, *Self and Society: A Symbolic Interactionist Social Psychology*, ninth ed. (Boston: Allyn and Bacon, 2003), 102.
6. Hewitt, *Self and Society*, 111.
7. Hewitt, *Self and Society*, 111.
8. A. Strauss, *Mirrors and Masks: The Search for Identity* (San Francisco: Sociology Press, 1959).
9. P. Biernacki, *Pathways from Heroin Addiction: Recovery without Treatment* (Philadelphia: Temple University Press, 1986), 141.
10. D. Waldorf, C. Reinarman, and S. Murphy, *Cocaine Changes: The Experience of Using and Quitting* (Philadelphia: Temple University Press, 1991), 223.
11. H. Becker, "Notes on the Concept of Commitment," *American Journal of Sociology* 66 (1960): 32–42.
12. Becker, "Notes on the Concept of Commitment," 32–42.
13. C. Terry, *The Fellas: Overcoming Prison and Addiction* (Belmont, CA: Wadsworth/Thomson Learning, 2003).
14. D. Rudy, *Becoming Alcoholic: Alcoholics Anonymous and the Reality of Alcoholism* (Carbondale: Southern Illinois University Press, 1986).
15. J. McIntosh and N. McKeganey, *Beating the Dragon: The Recovery from Dependent Drug Use* (Harlow, England: Prentice Hall, 2002).
16. H. Blumer, *Symbolic Interactionism: Perspective and Method* (Englewood Cliffs, NJ: Prentice Hall, 1969); K. Sandstrom, D. Martin, and G. Fine, *Symbols, Selves, and Social Reality: A Symbolic Interactionist Approach to Social Psychology and Sociology* (Los Angeles: Roxbury, 2003).
17. Hewitt, *Self and Society;* G. H. Mead, *Mind, Self and Society from the Standpoint of a Social Behaviorist*, ed. C. Morris (Chicago: University of Chicago Press, 1934).
18. Hewitt, *Self and Society.*
19. V. Vinitzky-Seroussi and R. Zussman, "High School Reunions and the Management of Identity" *Symbolic Interaction* 19 (1996): 225–29.
20. J. Hewitt, *Dilemmas of the American Self* (Philadelphia: Temple University Press, 1989), 183.
21. J. Haas, *Seeking Bliss: The Study of Addiction and Recovery* (Victoria, British Columbia: Mosaic, 2003), 60.
22. N. Denzin, *The Recovering Alcoholic* (Newbury Park, CA: Sage, 1987).

23. Denzin, *Recovering Alcoholic.*

24. S. Brown, *Treating the Alcoholic.*

25. S. Brown, *Treating the Alcoholic;* Denzin, *Recovering Alcoholic.*

26. S. Maruna, *Making Good: How Ex-Convicts Reform and Rebuild Their Lives* (Washington, DC: American Psychological Association, 2001).

27. Maruna, *Making Good;* T. Meisenhelder, "Becoming Normal: Certification as a Stage in Exiting from Crime," *Criminology* 15 (1982): 319–34.

28. Maruna, *Making Good,* 156.

29. Maruna, *Making Good,* 158.

30. C. Cooley, "The Social Self," in *Social Deviance: Readings in Theory and Research,* ed. H. Pontell (Englewood Cliffs, NJ: Prentice Hall, 1996), 63.

31. Terry, *Fellas,* 12.

32. Maruna, *Making Good,* 158.

33. Denzin, *Recovering Alcoholic.*

34. Mead, *Mind, Self and Society from the Standpoint of a Social Behaviorist,* 90.

35. Denzin, *Recovering Alcoholic,* 190.

36. McIntosh and McKeganey, *Beating the Dragon.*

37. Denzin, *Recovering Alcoholic;* McIntosh and McKeganey, *Beating the Dragon.*

38. Maruna, *Making Good,* 156; Terry, *Fellas.*

39. Maruna, *Making Good,* 119.

40. K. Kiecolt, "Stress and the Decision to Change Oneself: A Theoretical Model," *Social Psychological Quarterly* 57 (1994): 61.

41. E. Lewin, "By Design: Reproductive Strategies and the Meaning of Motherhood," in *The Sexual Politics of Reproduction,* ed. H. Homans (Albershot, England: Gower, 1985), 125.

42. Brown, *Treating the Alcoholic;* M. Rosenbaum, *Women on Heroin* (New Brunswick, NJ: Rutgers University Press, 1981); R. Stevens, *The Street Addict Role: A Theory of Heroin Addiction* (Albany: State University of New York Press, 1991); Terry, *Fellas.*

43. Brown, *Treating the Alcoholic;* Terry, *Fellas.*

44. Maruna, *Making Good,* 153; Biernacki, *Pathways from Heroin Addiction.*

45. Maruna, *Making Good,* 153.

46. I. Janis and L. Mann, *Decision Making: A Psychological Analysis of Conflict, Choice, and Commitment* (New York: Free Press, 1977); J. Prochaska, J. Norcross, and C. DiClemente, *Changing for Good: A Revolutionary Six-Change Program for Overcoming Bad Habits and Moving Your Life Positively Forward* (New York: Avon, 1994); Stevens, *Street Addict Role.*

47. J. O. Prochaska and C. DiClemente, "Toward a Comprehensive Model of Change," in *Treating Addictive Behaviors: Processes of Change,* ed. W. R. Miller and N. Heather, Applied Clinical Psychology Series (New York: Plenum, 1986): 3–27; J. O. Prochaska, C. DiClemente, and J. C. Norcross, "In Search of How People Change: Applications to Addictive Behaviors," *American Psychologist* 47 (1992): 1101–14; Prochaska, Norcross, and DiClemente, *Changing for Good.*

48. Prochaska, Norcross, and DiClemente, *Changing for Good,* 48.

49. Prochaska, Norcross, and DiClemente, *Changing for Good,* 48.

50. Prochaska, Norcross, and DiClemente, *Changing for Good,* 48.

51. Prochaska, Norcross, and DiClemente, *Changing for Good,* 48.

52. R. Granfield and W. Cloud, *Coming Clean: Overcoming Addiction without Treatment* (New York: New York University Press, 1999), 97.

53. J. Leibrich, *Straight to the Point: Angles on Giving up Crime* (Otago, New Zealand: University of Otago Press, 1993), 51.

54. Maruna, *Making Good,* 126.

55. H. Whitmore, "Hitting Bottom Can Be the Beginning," *Parade Magazine,* March 15, 1992, 5.

56. Brown, *Treating the Alcoholic*, 18.

57. Brown, *Treating the Alcoholic*, 18.

58. S. Henry, "Newsmaking Criminology as Replacement Discourse," in *Media, Process and the Social Construction of Crime: Studies in Newsmaking Criminology*, ed. G. Barak (New York: Garland, 1994), 299.

59. Maruna, *Making Good*, 114

60. Maruna, *Making Good*, 114.

61. J. Braithwaite and S. Mugford, "Conditions of Successful Reintegration Ceremonies: Dealing with Juvenile Offenders," *British Journal of Criminology* 34 (1994): 148.

62. E. O'Reilly, *Sobering Tales: Narratives of Alcoholism and Recovery* (Amherst: University of Massachusetts Press, 1997), 23.

63. H. Becker, B. Geer, E. Hughes, and A. Strauss, *Boys in White: Student Culture in Medical School* (Chicago: University of Chicago Press, 1992).

64. Waldorf, Reinarman, and Murphy, *Cocaine Changes*, 223.

65. R. Flacks, *Making History: The American Left and the American Mind* (New York: Columbia University Press, 1988), 2.

Chapter 5

Conclusion

Introduction

In the preceding chapters, I explored women's perspectives of how they begin to engage with addiction to alcohol and/or drugs, how they process addiction experiences, and how they disengage from their use of substances. Such an exploration provides important insights into how these twenty-five rural women made meanings of these experiences. As Hewitt argues:

> There is in symbolic interactionism the underlying idea that people are not stamped out by their environment or by their socializers, that regardless of how others define us, there is also the fact that individuals will interact with themselves, develop their own identities apart from others, overcoming in part the power of social interaction.[1]

The women I interviewed for this study echoed Theresa's comment: "I do not necessarily have to be who I have learned from others I am." Through their new definitions of selves and social identities, they found real alternatives by which they could guide their lives and continue in a new direction.

Much of the literature follows a common theme: self and identity changes are fundamental in both addiction and recovery processes.[2] What is specifically missing from the literature, however, is an elaboration on the relationship between rural Appalachian women's alcohol and/or drug use and the ways in which they generate new selves and social identities as they process these changes.[3] As Ferguson argues, "Nearly all feminists agree that women have historically been denied the opportunity to construct their own separate identity, their own sense of selfhood and purpose apart from the definitions imposed on them by men."[4] Therefore, this study seeks to analyze the relationship between rural Appalachian women's alcohol and/or drug use and their agency as they construct new social and individual identities and move between addiction and recovery. Understanding how women experience these changes provides a more comprehensive view of such issues and offers practical suggestions for outreach and treatment programs for women.

Women have different life experiences, and rural Appalachian women experience life differently, as this study has shown. This variation has given rise to different, but equally valid, interpretations for those experiences.[5] The personal testimonies of my participants enlarge the overall scope of knowledge of rural women's recovery processes. Because the study materials consist of retrospective information, I cannot state with certainty whether participants will stay in their recovery. Still, it is also clear that these women broke their processes of addiction for lengths of time and that they have substantially changed their lives.

The world of rural Appalachian women has not been discussed widely and is not known by those within the addiction and recovery fields to any great extent—unless they specifically seek to know. I argue that we need to encourage rural women to speak and to find words for their experiences. In doing so, rural women will be recognized as important partners in civilized society.[6] As more scholars consider women's lives in their research, what women do will matter, what women are will matter, and how women relate with each other and with men will matter. Crooks argues that "[a]s women gain their voice and collectively create a history accessible to all, they will take control of their lives."[7]

Participants had various strengths, including courage, honesty, hope, perseverance, resourcefulness, planning for the future, work ethics, and responsibilities.[8] The possession of such strengths gave rise to a sense of confidence and a perception of self-efficacy for participants.[9]

Using a symbolic interactionist paradigm coupled with a feminist perspective enables me to understand how participants see themselves and how they actualize and change the social construction of their addiction and recovery processes. By changing meanings toward themselves and toward the objects of interest, alcohol and/or drugs, participants empowered themselves as they changed their lives.

Symbolic interactionism views the self as a social force in its own right. Socialization endows the individual with the capacity to cooperate in social acts with others; but the individual is not an automaton who unfailingly reproduces the meanings and actions she or he has been taught. It is the individual who acts, who does the interpreting, naming, and coordinating that permit joint actions to proceed or that disrupt or derail them.[10] To have a self is to choose, to decide, to exert control over one's own conduct and that of others. The existence of a self endows the individual actor with the capacity to recognize and act in the pursuit of self-interest and, most importantly, to conceive of herself or himself in opposition to the social world and not just as dependent on it. The sentient being is as much responsible for the creation of the self as is the surrounding social world. Most importantly, "[t]hrough their capacity to rebel, to innovate, to resist social influences, and to apply social knowledge creatively in an effort to solve problems, individuals make felt their influence on the social world."[11]

Overall, participants in this study are potential innovators, inventors, and creators of new forms of conduct for themselves.[12]

A Personal Narrative

In some ways, this was a difficult study to write. The interviews I conducted with my participants were filled with stories of poignancy and courage, similar to those of the Canadian women I previously had worked with on the Women and Substance Abuse (*WASA*) Project. But the lives of the rural Appalachian women differed in one significant way from those of the women in Canada with whom I had worked. The area in which the rural participants lived is extremely poor and underdeveloped; there are only limited resources for women in recovery. Although there is one center that attempts to help women who are addicted, there is no provision for follow-up after they leave the program. For these women, there is little in the way of unemployment assistance, educational help, or daycare for them and their children.

Many of the women I interviewed were dealing not only with their own recovery but also with violence and sexual abuse in their lives. For these women, then, double jeopardy was in play: recovery along with continuing personal violence and abuse. It became obvious to me that, in order for these women to recover, they needed considerable personal courage, tenacity, and strength—attributes that my participants displayed throughout the interviews.

After each interview I wrote field notes, then put them aside. After I transcribed the interviews, I referred back to these notes to refresh my memory as I began to analyze the women's narratives. I thought back to how my participants had talked about their preaddiction experiences and their immersion in their addictive lifestyles. My two data chapters, "The Preaddicted Self" and "The Addicted Self," were particularly difficult for me to write. In these two chapters, the women's interviews were dark, foreboding, and full of pain. I could feel the grief in their voices as I transcribed their narratives. Looking back at my notes, I read again what I had written about how the women talked to me: how their body language and their voices showed how they felt about relating those experiences to me. The participants talked in soft, low voices, did not look at me in many cases, and remained stooped in their chairs. There was no vivacity viability and seemingly no hope in their voices as they spoke.

Conversely, as participants talked about recovering selves, their language changed: their voices were filled with joy, and there was a sense of passion as they recounted their successes. Some women even showed palpable anger as they told their recovery stories. The participants' body language changed radically: they sat up in their chairs, they looked me square in the eye, and their voices were raised, full of expectations and optimism. It was obvious to me that the women finally loved themselves and their recovering lives. The last data chapter, "The Recovering Self," literally wrote itself—I found it easy to write because it showed participants' happiness in their recovery as their sense of aspirations and delight came through in the transcripts.

Although I found many aspects of these women's lives difficult to hear, transcribe, and analyze, their stories of resistance and courage give me hope for other women in similar situations. Writing this study, trying as it was at times, was a delight: it enabled me to counter the selective inattention of extant research toward formerly addicted rural women's experiences. The participants' survival strategies brought out hidden strengths deep inside themselves, their capacities to learn to live again in their recovery, and their abilities to enhance their diminished sense of selves. I feel honored and privileged to have had the opportunity to document these twenty-five rural Appalachian women's stories of recovery from their former addictive lives.

Suggestions for Change

In a practical manner, what suggestions can be made in terms of policy to the substantive focus of this study—rural Appalachian women who were formerly addicted to alcohol and/or drugs? Each woman's account offered insights into further recommendations that evolve from this study. The following discussion highlights these recommendations.

There is a need to validate rural women's experiential knowledge as "knowing agents" in their addiction and recovery processes. A key necessity is a policy base that respects women's differences and women's knowledge production. A respect for their multiple voices is needed, along with an integration of their legitimacy in policy making. Rural women's addiction and recovery needs to be situated in the context of women's subordination and social constraints. Policy work should take into account that women suffer greater social exclusion, stigma, and isolation than do male addicts in addiction and recovery.

Policy work should strengthen rural women's economic security, their right to education, access to proper childcare, health care, and reproductive rights. Increased spending at the community level for these factors should be implemented more thoroughly. A sparse population limits the number and assortment of services that can be offered in a given region. The per capita costs of providing special services often make them too expensive to implement. Yet cost does not lessen the need for those kinds of services by the people who live in a rural area.[13]

Researchers should integrate theory and praxis when working with rural women as they process their addiction and recovery. Treatment programs should integrate a more holistic theory of women's lives into training modules for counselors and therapists in addiction and community centers. Addiction centers and shelters need to work together in validating rural women's experiences of alcohol and/or drug use and violence in their lives. Feelings of isolation, lack of health insurance and continuity of care, lack of transportation, as well as heightened concerns about confidentiality may exacerbate the problem of domestic violence in rural areas.[14] Because women in shelters and women in addiction centers may be using alcohol and/or drugs in order to cope with former or present violence in their lives, work on violence issues should be of primary concern before women's addiction/recovery issues are considered.

Furthermore, according to the American Psychological Association,[15] in rural areas the barriers to people seeking mental health care may be similar to those in urban areas: the perceived stigma associated with mental illness, lack of understanding about mental illnesses and their treatments, lack of information about where to go for treatment, and the inability to pay for care. However, in rural areas where "everyone knows everyone," the lack of anonymity can be an additional barrier. Geographical distances, lack of transportation, and cost of mental health care services as well as lack of insurance and maldistribution of providers can be additional obstacles to rural women accessing such care.[16]

In conclusion, I offer the following suggestions for further research on the issues of rural women's addiction/recovery processes. First, more research needs to be undertaken in order to enrich the literature on rural women's addiction and recovery processes. As stated earlier, most empirical research on women gives very little information about rural women's true consciousness or rural women's individual and social history. Therefore, more attention should be focused on rural women's experiences in order to continue to close the gap in the literature that heretofore has considered a "masculinist"[17] truth about such processes. More research is needed that considers either a convergence or divergence between urban and rural women and between rural women and rural men. Through bringing rural women's experiences into the description of social life a necessary balance to scientific inquiry is generated.

Second, little is known about how rural women, in particular, start and stop their use of alcohol and/or drugs. Therefore, future research should consider such self changes as individuals process these experiences. As Fine argues, "Knowledge is best gathered in the midst of social change projects. Such research is important as it is at once disruptive, transformative, and reflective; about understanding and about action; not about freezing the change but always about change."[18]

Third, as Ettorre argues, the development of a gender-sensitive perspective on addiction/recovery remains in "the infancy stage."[19] Therefore, more studies would contribute to filling this lack in the literature and research fields. Finally, most addiction/recovery studies do not consider individuals' subjective experiences.[20] It must be remembered that "[t]he individual is a participant in that interaction as much as anyone else involved."[21]

Women have different life experiences, and women experience life differently, as this study has shown. This has given rise to different, but equally valid, interpretations for those experiences.[22] The personal testimonies of my participants are a source that enlarges the overall scope of knowledge of addiction and recovery processes. As one participant stated as she explained her recovery, "I can see more clearly." My hope for this research is that, through my participants' voices, I have provided a picture of formerly addicted rural Appalachian women's experiences that will help us to see more clearly their lives, their needs, and their concerns.

Notes

1. J. Hewitt, *Self and Society: A Symbolic Interactionist Social Psychology,* ninth ed. (Boston: Allyn and Bacon, 2003), 266.

2. H. Becker, *Outsiders* (New York: Free Press, 1963); N. Denzin, *The Alcoholic Self* (Newbury Park, CA: Sage, 1987); N. Denzin, *The Recovering Alcoholic* (Newbury Park, CA: Sage, 1987); R. Granfield and W. Cloud, *Coming Clean: Overcoming Addiction without Treatment* (New York University Press, 1999); J. Haas, *Seeking Bliss: The Study of Addiction and Recovery* (Victoria, British Columbia: Mosaic, 2003); A. Lindesmith, *Addiction and Opiates* (Chicago: Aldine, 1968).

3. N. Campbell, *Gender, Drug Policy, and Social Justice: Using Women* (New York: Routledge, 2000); E. Ettorre, *Women and Substance Use* (London: Macmillan, 1992); J. Gurin, "Remaking our Lives," *American Health* 9 (1990): 50–52; S. Murphy and M. Rosenbaum, *Pregnant Women on Drugs: Combating Stereotypes and Stigma* (New Brunswick, NJ: Rutgers University Press, 1999); P. Raine, *Women's Perspectives on Drugs and Alcohol: The Vicious Circle* (Hampshire, England: Ashgate, 2001); M. Rosenbaum, *Women on Heroin* (New Brunswick, NJ: Rutgers University Press, 1981); M. Rosenbaum, *Women and Drugs: Twenty-five Years of Research and Policy* (San Francisco: Lindesmith Center, 1998).

4. K. Ferguson, *Self, Society, and Womankind* (Westport, CT: Greenwood, 1980).

5. M. Fine, *Disruptive Voices: The Possibilities of Feminist Research* (Ann Arbor: University of Michigan Press, 1992), 128–29.

6. D. Crooks, "The Importance of Symbolic Interaction in Grounded Theory Research on Women's Health," *Health Care for Women International* 22 (2001): 11–28.

7. Crooks, "Importance of Symbolic Interaction," 17.

8. B. Geiger and M. Fischer, "Female Repeat Offenders Negotiating Identity," *International Journal of Offender Therapy and Comparative Criminology* 47 (2003): 496–515.

9. A. Bandura, "Perceived Self-Efficacy in Cognitive Development and Functioning," *Educational Psychologist* 28 (1993): 117–48.

10. Hewitt, *Self and Society,* 262.

11. Hewitt, *Self and Society,* 262.

12. Hewitt, *Self and Society,* 262.

13. A. Bushy, *Proceedings from the National Rural Health Association Conference,* Kansas City, MO: Center for Health Economics Research, 1993.

14. R. Johnson, *Rural Health Responses to Domestic Violence: Policy and Practice Issues*, Office of Rural Health Policy, http://ruralhealth.hrsa.gov/pub/domviol.htm (September 1, 2005).

15. National Rural Health Association (NRHA), *Policy Brief,* November 2005.

16. NRHA, *Policy Brief.*

17. Ettorre, *Women and Substance Use,* 146.

18. Fine, *Disruptive Voices,* 227.

19. Ettorre, *Women and Substance Use,* 3.

20. J. McIntosh and N. McKeganey, *Beating the Dragon: The Recovery from Dependent Drug Use* (Harlow, England: Prentice Hall, 2002).

21. T. Anderson, "Identity Transformation in Drug Addiction" (PhD diss., American University, 1991), 351.

22. Fine, *Disruptive Voices,* 227.

Selected Bibliography

Abbot, A. A. "Substance Use and the Feminist Perspective." In *Feminist Practice in the 21st Century*, edited by N. Van Den Bergh, 258–78. Washington, DC: National Association of Social Workers Press, 1995.

Adrian, M., C. Lundy, and M. Eliany, eds. *Canadian Women and Substance Use: Overview and Policy Implications*. Toronto, Ontario: Addiction Research Foundation, 1996.

Akers, R., M. Kron, L. Lanza-Kaduse, and M. Radosevich. "Social Learning and Deviant Behavior: A Specific Test of a General Theory." *American Sociological Review* 44 (1979): 636–55.

Anderson, K., and D. C. Jack. "Learning to Listen: Interview Techniques and Analyses." In *Women's Words: The Feminist Practice of Oral History*, edited by S. B. Gluck and D. Patai, 11–26. New York: Routledge, 1991.

Anderson, T. "Identity Transformation in Drug Addiction." PhD diss., American University, 1991.

Bandura, A. "Perceived Self-Efficacy in Cognitive Development and Functioning." *Educational Psychologist* 28 (1993): 117–48.

Becker, H. "Becoming a Marijuana User." *American Journal of Sociology* 59 (1953): 235–42.

———. "Notes on the Concept of Commitment," *American Journal of Sociology* 66 (1960): 32–42.

———. *Outsiders*. New York: Free Press, 1963.

Becker, H., B. Geer, E. Hughes, and A. Strauss. *Boys in White: Student Culture in Medical School*. Chicago: University of Chicago Press, 1992.

Beckman, L. "Self-Esteem of Women Alcoholics." *Journal of Studies on Alcohol* 39 (1978): 491–98.

Bernard, W. T. *Including Black Women in Health and Social Policy Development: Winning over Addictions; Empowering Black Mothers with Addictions to Overcome Triple Jeopardy*. Halifax, Nova Scotia: Maritime Centre of Excellence for Women's Health, 2001.

Biernacki, P. *Pathways from Heroin Addiction: Recovery without Treatment*. Philadelphia: Temple University Press, 1986.

Blackwell, J., W. E. Thurston, and K. Graham. "Women's Use of Alcohol, Tobacco and Other Drugs in Canada." In *Canadian Women and Substance Use: Overview and Policy Implications*, edited by M. Adrian, C. Lundy, and M. Eliany, 228–46. Toronto, Ontario: Addiction Research Foundation, 1996.

Blood, L., and A. Cornwall. "Childhood Sexual Victimization as a Factor in the Treatment of Substance Misusing Adolescents." *Substance Use and Misuse* 31 (1996): 1015–39.

Blume, S. "Alcohol and Drug Problems in Women: Old Attitudes, New Knowledge." In *Treatment Choices for Alcoholism and Substance Abuse*, edited by H. Milkman and L. Sederer, 183–98. Toronto, Ontario: Lexington Books, 1990.

Blumer, H. *Symbolic Interactionism: Perspective and Method.* Englewood Cliffs, NJ: Prentice Hall, 1969.

Blumer, H., A. Sutter, R. Smith, and S. Ahmed. *The World of Youthful Drug Use.* Berkeley: Regents of the University of California, 1967.

Bologh, R. W. "Feminist Social Theorizing and Moral Reasoning on Difference and Dialectic." In *Sociological Theory*, edited by R. Collins, 363–425. San Francisco: Jossey-Bass, 1983.

Braithwaite, J., and S. Mugford. "Conditions of Successful Reintegration Ceremonies: Dealing with Juvenile Offenders." *British Journal of Criminology* 34 (1994): 139–71.

Broadhead, R. *Inundation of Family Life: The Impact of Professional Socialization on the Families of Medical Students.* Los Angeles: University of California Press, 1978.

Brown, B. S., S. K. Gauvey, M. B. Myers, and S. D. Stark. "In Their Own Words: Addicts' Reasons for Initiating and Withdrawing from Heroin." *International Journal of the Addictions* 6 (1971): 635–45.

Brown, S. *Treating the Alcoholic: A Developmental Model of Recovery.* New York: John Wiley and Sons, 1985.

Brownfield, D. "Adolescent Male Status and Delinquent Behavior." *Sociological Spectrum* 10 (April–June 1990): 227–48.

Bureau of Justice Statistics. *Compendium of Federal Justice Statistics.* 2003.

———. *Women Offenders.* December 1999. http://www.ojp.usdoj.gov/bjs/ (6 Feb. 2007).

Bushy, A., ed. *Proceedings from the National Rural Health Association Conference.* Kansas City, MO: Center for Health Economics Research.

———. "Rural Women: Lifestyle and Health Status." *Rural Nursing* 28 (1993): 187–97.

Bynum, J., and W. Thompson. *Juvenile Delinquency: A Sociological Approach.* Sixth ed. Boston: Allyn and Bacon, 2005.

Campbell, N. *Gender, Drug Policy, and Social Justice: Using Women.* New York: Routledge, 2000.

Canadian Centre on Substance Abuse. "CCSA Canadian Profile." 1999. http://www.ccsa.ca/index.asp (November 19, 2004).

Celentano, D. D. and D. McQueen, "Multiple Substance Use among Women with Alcohol-Related problems." In *Alcohol Problems in Women*, edited by S. C. Wilsnack and L. J. Beckman, 97–116. New York: Guilford, 1984.

Centers for Disease Control. *Youth Risk Behavior Surveillance, United States, 2003* 53 (2004): 1–96.

———. *HIV and AIDS—United States, 1981–2001* 50 (2001): 430–34.

———. *HIV/AIDS Surveillance Report, Year End Edition.* 2001. http://www.cdc.gov/hiv/topics/surveillance/resources/reports/2003supp_vol9no2/default.htm (6 Feb. 2007).

Centre for Infectious Disease Prevention and Control, Health Canada. *National HIV Prevalence and Incidence Estimates for 1999: No Evidence of a Decline in Overall Incidence.* http://www.phac-aspc.gc.ca/publicat/epiu-aepi/hiv-vih/estima_e.html (6 Feb. 2007).

Chafetz, J. S. *Feminist Sociology: An Overview of Contemporary Theories.* Itasca, IL: F. E. Peacock Publishers, 1988.

Charon, J. *Symbolic Interactionism: An Introduction, an Interpretation, an Integration.* Seventh ed. Upper Saddle River, NJ: Prentice Hall, 2001.

Clark, J. "The Historical Context of Medicalization and Gender: Its Relationship to Alcohol and Other Drug Use in Canada." In *Women's Use of Alcohol, Tobacco and Other Drugs in Canada*, edited by M. Adrian, C. Lundy, and M. Eliany, 14–20. Toronto, Ontario: Addiction Research Foundation, 1996.

Code, L. *What Can She Know? Feminist Theory and the Construction of Knowledge.* Ithaca, NY: Cornell University Press, 1991.

Cohen, A. Y. "Inside What's Happening: Sociological, Psychological, and Spiritual Perspectives on the Contemporary Drug Scene." *American Journal of Public Health* 59 (1969): 2092–95.

Cohen, P. "Cocaine Use in Amsterdam in Non-deviant Subcultures." Paper presented at the International Council on Alcohol and Addictions Congress, Lausanne, Switzerland, June 1987.

Collins, P. H. *Black Feminist Thought: Knowledge, Consciousness, and the Politics of Empowerment.* New York: Routledge, 1990.

Comack, E. *Women in Trouble.* Halifax, Nova Scotia: Fernwood, 1996.

Cooley, C. "The Social Self." In *Social Deviance: Readings in Theory and Research,* edited by H. Pontell, 51–53. Englewood Cliffs, NJ: Prentice Hall, 1996.

Coombs, R., L. J. Fry, and P. G. Lewis, eds. *Socialization in Drug Use.* Cambridge, MA: Schenkman, 1976.

Copeland, J. "A Qualitative Study of Self-Managed Change in Substance Dependence among Women." *Contemporary Drug Problems* 25 (Summer 1998): 321–43.

Crooks, D. "The Importance of Symbolic Interaction in Grounded Theory Research on Women's Health." *Health Care for Women International* 22 (2001): 11–28.

DeKeseredy, W., M. D. Schwartz, D. Fagen, and M. Hall. "Separation/Divorce Sexual Assault: The Contribution of Male Support." *Feminist Criminology* 1 (July 2006): 228–50.

Dell, C. A., and K. Garabedian. *Canadian Community Epidemiology Network on Drug Use: 2002 National Report.* Ottawa, Ontario: Canadian Center on Substance Use, 2003.

Denzin, N. *The Alcoholic Self.* Newbury Park, CA: Sage, 1987.

———. *The Recovering Alcoholic.* Newbury Park, CA: Sage, 1987.

———. *Symbolic Interactionism and Cultural Studies: The Politics of Interpretation.* Oxford: Blackwell, 1992.

Department of Health and Human Services. *Alcohol and Health: Seventh Report to Congress.* Rockville, MD: Department of Health and Human Services, 1990.

Donnermeyer, J. F. "The Use of Alcohol, Marijuana, and Hard Drugs by Rural Adolescents: A Review of Recent Research." *Drugs and Society* 50 (1992): 31–77.

Duongsaa, U. "Women, Gender and Drugs." Speech presented to UNDP Panel Discussion on Drugs and Development at the United Nations General Assembly Special Session on Drugs, New York, June 1998.

Ebaugh, H. R. F. *Becoming an Ex: The Process of Role-Exit.* Chicago: University of Chicago Press, 1988.

Elliott, P., and N. Mandell. "Feminist Theories." In *Feminist Issues: Race, Class, and Sexuality*, edited by N. Mandell, 3–31. Scarborough, Ontario: Prentice Hall Canada, 1995.

Ettorre, E. *Women and Substance Use.* London: Macmillan, 1992.

Faupel, C., A. Hortowitz, and G. Weaver. *The Sociology of American Drug Use.* Boston: McGraw-Hill, 2004.

Feldman, D. J., and H. S. Feldman. "On the Etiology of Narcotic Addiction and Its Relation to Curiosity." *Psychosomatics* 13 (1972): 304–8.

Feldman, H. "Ideological Supports to Becoming and Remaining a Heroin Addict." *Journal of Health and Social Behavior* 9 (1968): 131–39.

Ferguson, K. *Self, Society, and Womankind.* Westport, CT: Greenwood, 1980.
Ferree, M. M., J. Lorder, and B. B. Heiss. *Revisioning Gender.* Thousand Oaks, CA: Sage, 1999.
Fine, M. *Disruptive Voices: The Possibilities of Feminist Research.* Ann Arbor: University of Michigan Press, 1992.
Flacks, R. *Making History: The American Left and the American Mind.* New York: Columbia University Press, 1988.
Franz, C., and A. Stewart. *Women Creating Lives: Identities, Resilience and Resistance.* Boulder, CO: Westview, 1994.
Gagne, P. L. "Appalachian Women: Violence and Social Control." *Journal of Contemporary Ethnography* 20 (1992): 387–415.
Gannon, J. P. *Soul Survivors: A New Beginning for Adults Abused as Children.* New York: Prentice Hall, 1989.
Garfinkel, H. *Studies in Ethnomethodology.* Englewood Cliffs, NJ: Prentice Hall, 1967.
Geiger, B., and M. Fischer. "Female Repeat Offenders Negotiating Identity." *International Journal of Offender Therapy and Comparative Criminology* 47 (2003): 496–515.
Giddens, A. *The Constitution of Society.* Cambridge, MA: Polity Press, 1984.
Gilligan, C. *In a Different Voice: Psychological Theory and Women's Development.* Cambridge, MA: Harvard University Press, 1993.
Glaser, B., and A. Strauss. *The Discovery of Grounded Theory: Strategies for Qualitative Research.* Chicago: Aldine, 1967.
Goode, E. *Drugs in American Society.* Fifth ed. Boston: McGraw-Hill, 1999.
Gorham, L. "The Growing Problem of Low Earnings in Rural Areas." In *Rural Poverty in America*, edited by C. Duncan, 21–40. New York: Auburn House, 1992.
Graham, H. "Surveying through Stories." In *Social Researching: Politics, Problems, Practice,* edited by C. Bell and H. Roberts, 104–24. London: Routledge, 1984.
Graham, K., V. Carver, and P. J. Brett. "Alcohol and Drug Use by Older Women: Results of a National Survey." *Canadian Journal of Aging* 14 (1995): 769–91.
Granfield, R., and W. Cloud. *Coming Clean: Overcoming Addiction without Treatment.* New York: New York University Press, 1999.
Grant, J. *The Women and Substance Abuse Report (WASA): The Invisible Problem.* Moncton, New Brunswick: Support to Single Parents, 1997.
Grella, C., and V. Joshi. "Gender Differences in Drug Treatment Careers among Clients in the National Drug Use Treatment Outcome Study." *American Journal of Drug and Alcohol Use* 25 (1999): 385.
Grover, S. M., and S. P. Thomas. "Substance Use and Anger in Mid-life Women." *Issues in Mental Health Nursing* 14 (1993): 19–29.
Gurin, J. "Remaking Our Lives." *American Health* 9 (1990): 50–52.
Haas, J. *Seeking Bliss: The Study of Addiction and Recovery.* Victoria, British Columbia: Mosaic, 2003.
Harding, S. *Feminism and Methodology.* Bloomington: Indiana University Press, 1987.
Heitzeg, N. *Deviance: Rulemakers and Rulebreakers.* Minneapolis, MN: West, 1996.
Henry, S. "Newsmaking Criminology as Replacement Discourse." In *Media, Process and the Social Construction of Crime: Studies in Newsmaking Criminology*, edited by G. Barak, 287–318. New York: Garland, 1994.
Hewitt, J. *Dilemmas of the American Self.* Philadelphia: Temple University Press, 1989.
———. *Self and Society: A Symbolic Interactionist Social Psychology.* Ninth ed. Boston: Allyn and Bacon, 2003.
Hoff, L. A. *Battered Women as Survivors.* London: Routledge, 1990.
Horne, T. *Making a Difference: Program Evaluation for Health Promotion.* Edmonton, Alberta: WellQuest Consulting, 1995.

Janis, I., and L. Mann. *Decision Making: A Psychological Analysis of Conflict, Choice, and Commitment.* New York: Free Press, 1977.

Johnson, R. "Rural Health Responses to Domestic Violence: Policy and Practice Issues." *Office of Rural Health Policy.* 2000. http://ruralhealth.hrsa.gov/pub/domviol.htm (1 Sept. 2005).

Josselson, R. *Revising Herself: The Story of Women's Identity from College to Midlife.* San Francisco: Jossey-Bass, 1996.

Kandel, D. "Inter- and Intragenerational Influences on Adolescent Marijuana Use." *Journal of Social Issues* 30 (1974): 107–35.

———. "On Processes of Peer Influence in Adolescent Drug Use: A Developmental Perspective," Advances in Alcohol and Substance Use 4 (Spring–Summer 1985): 139–63.

Kaschak, E. *Engendered Lives: A New Psychology of Women's Experiences.* New York: Basic Books, 1992.

Keeler, M. "Motivation for Marijuana Use: A Correlate of Adverse Reactions." *American Journal of Psychiatry* 125 (1968): 142–46.

Kendall, D. *Sociology in Our Times: The Essentials.* Fourth ed. Belmont, CA: Wadsworth/Thomson Learning, 2004.

Kiecolt, K. "Stress and the Decision to Change Oneself: A Theoretical Model." *Social Psychological Quarterly* 57 (1994): 49–63.

Kirby, S., and K. McKenna. *Experience, Research, Social Change: Methods from the Margins.* Toronto, Ontario: Garamond, 1989.

Lammers, S. M. M., D. E. H. Mainzer, and H. M. M. Breteler. "Submission and Rebellion: Excessive Drinking of Women in Problematic Heterosexual Partner Relationships." *International Journal of the Addictions* 30 (1995): 901–17.

Leibrich, J. *Straight to the Point: Angles on Giving up Crime.* Otago, New Zealand: University of Otago Press, 1993.

Lentin, R. "I'll Be a Post-Feminist in Post-Patriarchy: Reflexivity Is a Feminist Issue." http://www.iol.ie/~mazzoldi/toolsforchange/postmet/feminist.html (16 November 2004).

Lerner, G. *The Creation of Feminist Consciousness: From the Middle Ages to Eighteen-Seventy.* New York: Oxford University Press, 1993.

Levesque-Lopman, L. *Claiming Reality: Phenomenology and Women's Experience.* Totowa, NJ: Rowman and Littlefield, 1988.

Levine, L. *Codependent Forevermore.* Chicago: University of Chicago Press, 1999.

Lewin, E. "By Design: Reproductive Strategies and the Meaning of Motherhood." In *The Sexual Politics of Reproduction*, edited by H. Homans, 123–38. Albershot, England: Gower, 1985.

Li, P. *Social Research Methods: An Introduction.* Toronto, Ontario: Butterworth, 1981.

Lindesmith, A. *Addiction and Opiates.* Chicago: Aldine, 1968.

Lindesmith, A., A. Strauss, and N. Denzin. *Social Psychology.* New York: Holt, Rinehart, and Winston, 1977.

Long, A., and B. Mullen, "An Exploration of Women's Perceptions of the Major Factors That Contributed to Their Alcohol Abuse." *Journal of Advanced Nursing* 19 (1994): 623–39.

Mandell, N. Introduction to *Feminist Issues: Race, Class, and Sexuality*, edited by N. Mandell, vii–xxi. Scarborough, Ontario: Prentice Hall Canada, 1995.

Maruna, S. *Making Good: How Ex-Convicts Reform and Rebuild Their Lives.* Washington, DC: American Psychological Association, 2001.

Maxwell, J. *Qualitative Research Design: An Interactive Approach.* Thousand Oaks, CA: Sage, 1996.

McGee, Z. T. "Social Class Differences in Parental and Peer Influence on Adolescent Drug Use." *Deviant Behavior* 13 (October–December 1992): 349–72.

McIntosh, J., and N. McKeganey. *Beating the Dragon: The Recovery from Dependent Drug Use.* Harlow, England: Prentice Hall, 2002.

McMahon, M. *Engendering Motherhood: Identity and Self-Transformation in Women's Lives.* New York: Guilford, 1995.

Mead, G. H. *Mind, Self and Society.* Chicago: University of Chicago Press, 1962.

———. *Mind, Self and Society from the Standpoint of a Social Behaviorist.* Edited by C. Morris. Chicago: University of Chicago Press, 1934.

———. *The Philosophy of the Act.* University of Chicago Press, 1938.

Meisenhelder, T. "Becoming Normal: Certification as a Stage in Exiting from Crime." *Criminology* 15 (1982): 319–34.

Miller, B. A., and W. R. Downs. "The Impact of Family Violence on the Use of Alcohol by Women." *Alcohol Health and Research World* 17 (1993): 137–43.

Minister, K. "A Feminist Frame for the Oral History Interview." In *Women's Words: The Feminist Practice of Oral History*, edited by S. B. Gluck and D. Patai, 27–41. New York: Routledge, 1991.

Minzner, G. L., J. T. Barker, and P. H. Werme. "Patterns of Drug Use among College Students: A Preliminary Report." *American Journal of Psychiatry* 127 (1970): 15–24.

Murphy, S., and M. Rosenbaum. *Pregnant Women on Drugs: Combating Stereotypes and Stigma.* New Brunswick, NJ: Rutgers University Press, 1999.

Office of National Drug Policy. *The Escalating Costs of Drug Abuse in the U.S., 1992–2002.* Washington, DC: Office of National Drug Control Policy, 2001.

O'Reilly, E. *Sobering Tales: Narratives of Alcoholism and Recovery.* Amherst: University of Massachusetts Press, 1997.

Peele, S. *The Diseasing of America: Addiction Treatment out of Control.* Lexington, MA: Lexington Books, 1989.

Personal Narratives Group, ed. *Interpreting Women's Lives: Feminist Theory and Personal Narratives.* Bloomington: Indiana University Press, 1989.

Plant, M. *Women and Alcohol: Contemporary and Historical Perspectives.* London: Free Association Books, 1997.

Portnoy, B. "Healthy People in Rural America by the Year 2000." In *Sowing Seeds in the Mountains: Community-Based Coalitions for Cancer Prevention and Control,* edited by R. A. Couto, N. K. Simpson, and G. Harris, 102–19. Bethesda, MD: National Institutes of Health, 1995.

Prochaska, J. O., and C. DiClemente. "Toward a Comprehensive Model of Change." In *Treating Addictive Behaviors: Processes of Change*, edited by W. R. Miller and N. Heather, 3–27. Applied Clinical Psychology Series. New York: Plenum, 1986.

Prochaska, J. O., C. DiClemente, and J. C. Norcross. "In Search of How People Change: Applications to Addictive Behaviors." *American Psychologist* 47 (1992): 1101–14.

Prochaska, J., J. Norcross, and C. DiClemente. *Changing for Good: A Revolutionary Six-Change Program for Overcoming Bad Habits and Moving Your Life Positively Forward.* New York: Avon, 1994.

Raine, P. *Women's Perspectives on Drugs and Alcohol: The Vicious Circle.* Hampshire, England: Ashgate, 2001.

Regoli, R., and J. Hewitt. *Delinquency in Society.* Fourth ed. Boston: McGraw-Hill, 2000.

Reinharz, S. *Feminist Methods in Social Research.* New York: Oxford University Press, 1992.

Ritzer, G. *Contemporary Sociological Theory.* Third ed. New York: McGraw-Hill, 1992.

Rosenbaum, M. *Women and Drugs: Twenty-five Years of Research and Policy.* San Francisco: Lindesmith Center, 1998.

———. *Women on Heroin.* New Brunswick, NJ: Rutgers University Press, 1981.

Rosswurm, M. A. "Illness Experiences and Health Recovery Behaviors of Patients in Southern Appalachia." *Western Journal of Nursing Research* 18 (1996): 44–61.

Rudy, D. *Becoming Alcoholic: Alcoholics Anonymous and the Reality of Alcoholism.* Carbondale: Southern Illinois University Press, 1986.

Ryan, V., and J. Popour. *Five-Year Women's Plan.* Developed by the Capitol Area Substance Use Commission for the Office of Substance Use, Michigan Department of Health, IV, 4c, IV, 12c, 1983.

Sandmaier, M. *The Invisible Alcoholics: Women and Alcohol Use in America.* New York: McGraw-Hill, 1980.

Sandstrom, K., D. Martin, and G. Fine. *Symbols, Selves, and Social Reality: A Symbolic Interactionist Approach to Social Psychology and Sociology.* Los Angeles: Roxbury, 2003.

Schwartz, H., and J. Jacobs. *Qualitative Sociology: A Method to the Madness.* New York: Macmillan, 1979.

Sev'er, A. *Fleeing the House of Horrors: Women Who Have Left Abusive Partners.* Toronto, Ontario: University of Toronto Press, 2002.

Shibutani, T. *Social Processes: An Introduction to Sociology.* Berkeley, CA: University of California, 1986.

———. *Society and Personality: An Interactionist Approach to Social Psychology* Englewood Cliffs, NJ: Prentice Hall, 1961.

Smith, D. *The Everyday World as Problematic: A Feminist Sociology.* Toronto, Ontario: University of Toronto Press, 1987.

———. *Writing the Social: Critique, Theory and Investigations.* Toronto, Ontario: University of Toronto Press, 1999.

Stensland, J., C. Mueller, and J. Sutton. "An Analysis of the Financial Conditions of Health Care Institutions in the Appalachian Region and Their Economic Impacts." Bethesda, MD: Appalachian Regional Commission, 2002.

Stevens, R. *The Street Addict Role: A Theory of Heroin Addiction.* Albany: State University of New York Press, 1991.

Stewart, A. "Toward a Feminist Strategy for Studying Women's Lives." In *Women Creating Lives: Identities, Resilience, and Resistance*, edited by C. Franz and A. Stewart, 11–35. Boulder, CO: Westview, 1994.

Stivers, C. "Reflections on the Role of Personal Narrative in Social Science." *Signs: Journal of Women in Culture and Society* 18 (1993): 408–25.

Strauss, A. *Mirrors and Masks: The Search for Identity.* San Francisco: Sociology Press, 1959.

Substance Abuse and Mental Health Services Administration. *Results from the 2003 National Survey on Drug Use and Health.* Washington, DC: Department of Health and Human Services, 2004.

Tatum, T. "Rural Women's Recovery Program and Women's Outreach." *Substance Abuse and Mental Health Services Administration.* http://www.treatment.org/TAPS/TAP17/tap17rural.html (May 16, 2006).

Terry, C. *The Fellas: Overcoming Prison and Addiction.* Belmont, CA: Wadsworth/Thomson Learning, 2003.

Ussher, J. "A Feminist Perspective." In *Living with Drink: Women Who Live with Problem Drinkers,* edited by R. Velleman, A. Copello, and J. Maslin, 150–62. London: Longman, 1998.

Van Den Bergh, N. "Having Bitten the Apple: A Feminist Perspective on Addictions." In *Feminist Perspectives on Addiction*, edited by N. Van Den Bergh, 3–30. New York: Springer, 1991.

Vinitzky-Seroussi, V., and R. Zussman, "High School Reunions and the Management of Identity." *Symbolic Interaction* 19 (1996): 225–29.

Waldorf, D., C. Reinarman, and S. Murphy. *Cocaine Changes: The Experience of Using and Quitting.* Philadelphia: Temple University Press, 1991.

Websdale, N. "Rural Woman Abuse: The Voices of Kentucky Women." In *Deviance and Deviants, An Anthology*, edited by R. Tewksbury and P. Gagne, 163–73. Los Angeles: Roxbury, 2000.

———. *Rural Women Battering and the Justice System: An Ethnography.* Thousand Oaks, CA: Sage, 1998.

Weisheit, R., D. Falcone, and E. R. Wells. "Community Policing in Small Town and Rural America." *Crime and Delinquency* 40 (1994): 549–67.

Whitmore, H. "Hitting Bottom Can Be the Beginning." *Parade Magazine,* March 15, 1992, 4–6.

Index

About the Author

Judith Grant received her Ph.D. in women's studies from York University in Toronto, Ontario, Canada. She obtained her M.A. from the University of Toronto and her B.A. from the University of New Brunswick. Her research interests include drugs and gender, women and addiction/recovery, violence against women, public policy issues, criminology, and qualitative research methods. Dr. Grant taught for nine years at Canadian universities followed by six years in the United States teaching sociology and criminology courses. Dr. Grant's international work has taken her to Southeast Asia (the Philippines and Sri Lanka), documenting gender analysis reports for Canadian agencies, and to Russia, where she presented research on Canadian laws on domestic violence to the Centres for Women, Family, and Gender Studies in both Moscow and St. Petersburg. Her current research project focuses on men's stories of addiction and recovery in the region of the Ozarks in the United States. She is presently teaching at the University of Ontario Institute of Technology in Oshawa, Ontario, Canada.